BOOST YOUR PENSION AND INCOME FROM PROPERTY

KAM DOVEDI

First published in 2014 by Premier Property Ventures (UK) Ltd, England.

Author's photograph by John Cassidy
www.theheadshotguy.co.uk

Author services by Pedernales Publishing, LLC
www.pedernalespublishing.com

Strategic Book Writing and Publishing Consultant: Kevin Bermingham
www.thesuccessfulauthor.com

British Library Cataloguing in Publication Data.

A catalogue record for this book is available from the British Library.

Paperback edition   ISBN 978-1-500722-83-8

It is always your footsteps.

You carry me always.

Thank you.

Kam Dovedi

DEDICATION

I would like to dedicate this book to my late grandmother Lakshmi Devi, who showed an outstanding strength of character throughout her life, having a will power of steel.

Overcoming life's obstacles with dignity, heart, and persistence. Always standing up for righteousness, and never faltering in the face of adversity. She became a widow at the age of 23, bringing up a four-year-old son while being six months' pregnant with my mother. Never marrying again. Fighting extreme poverty, in a little village in India.

She fought cancer three times. Living life to the full till her last breath.

Always showing me that my challenges in life are miniscule, and how blessed I am, helping me become the man I am today. I have yet to meet another person in my life with her strength and courage.

ACKNOWLEDGEMENTS

I would like to thank all the great mentors who have been in my life, and want to openly admit that I owe all that has been achieved to these great individuals.

CONTENTS

DEDICATION V

ACKNOWLEDGEMENTS VII

CHAPTER 1: CREATE THE LIFE OF YOUR DREAMS 3

    WHO IS THIS BOOK FOR? 4

    WHY SHOULD YOU INVEST IN PROPERTY? 4

    WHY DO I INVEST IN PROPERTY? 11

    HOW CAN INVESTING IN PROPERTY TRULY HELP YOU? 26

    KEY LEARNINGS 31

CHAPTER 2: WHAT YOU NEED TO KNOW TO BE A SUCCESSFUL PROPERTY INVESTOR **35**

    EFFECTIVE STRATEGY 35

    WINNING TEAM 46

    PROVEN SYSTEM 56

    KEY LEARNINGS 61

CHAPTER 3: ACQUIRING PROPERTY **65**

    THE ACT FORMULA 65

    FINDING THE RIGHT LOCATION 65

    ANALYSE PROFITABILITY 74

    ACQUIRE THE PROPERTY 77

    KEY LEARNINGS 88

CHAPTER 4: CONVERTING OR REFURBISHING A PROPERTY **93**

    PROPERTY CONVERSION 94

    PROPERTY REFURBISHMENT PROCESS 97

    HOW TO AVOID MISTAKES 107

    KEY LEARNINGS 112

CHAPTER 5: TENANTING PROPERTY **117**

    PROFILING TENANTS 118

    ACQUIRING TENANTS 126

    MANAGING TENANTS 135

    🔑 KEY LEARNINGS 142

CHAPTER 6: THREE APPROACHES TO BUILDING A SUCCESSFUL
PROPERTY PORTFOLIO **147**

    DO IT YOURSELF (DIY) 148

    DONE WITH YOU (DWY) 151

    DONE FOR YOU (DFY) 158

    🔑 KEY LEARNINGS 167

CHAPTER 7: SUMMARY **171**

    CREATE THE LIFE OF YOUR DREAMS 171

    WHAT YOU NEED TO KNOW TO BE A SUCCESSFUL PROPERTY
    INVESTOR 172

    ACQUIRING PROPERTY 173

    CONVERTING OR REFURBISHING A PROPERTY 173

    TENANTING PROPERTY 174

    THE THREE APPROACHES TO BUILDING A SUCCESSFUL PROPERTY
    PORTFOLIO 175

YOUR NEXT STEP **177**

SUCCESS STORIES **179**

ABOUT THE AUTHOR **185**

A PERSONAL STATEMENT BY THE AUTHOR **187**

CHAPTER 1

CREATE THE LIFE OF YOUR DREAMS

In our lifetime, we all strive to create the life of our dreams. We all want the time to spend with our family and friends, the ability to make the choices we want and ultimately live a life of freedom.

The reason why many people are not able to live the life of their dreams is because they are not financially secure; they may not have the income, or a long term wealth creation strategy.

This book will show you how you can ultimately live the life of your dreams through securing your financial future.

In order to achieve this, you will need to have an investment in place to give you a long term, reliable, and sustainable income that you can retire on.

That investment, if you're like me, is property. There are many reasons why property is the best asset class you could ever invest in, and at the same time there are three key reasons why you should be investing in property.

However, rather than just stating that property is fantastic, let us evaluate the facts to prove why property is truly a great asset class.

WHO IS THIS BOOK FOR?

I have written this book to help you take control of your financial future. You do not want to rely on your pension pot, or on your job – you want a safe, solid investment in the shape of property assets, which will allow you to have more time, more choices and ultimately more freedom in life.

If you are someone who wants a get rich quick scheme, or an overnight fix, this book is most definitely not for you. To become very wealthy in property, it is about staying in the 'game' for the medium to long term.

If you are someone who wants unrealistic returns, this is not for you.

This book is for you if you are looking for a residual income to boost or replace your income, to increase the income for your pension and to create substantial and sustainable wealth, a pot of money from investing in high capital growth areas.

WHY SHOULD YOU INVEST IN PROPERTY?

There are many reasons why property is one of the best asset classes to be investing in, but to truly show this, we will have to compare this investment with other traditional investments.

PROPERTY VS OTHER INVESTMENTS

The first type of investment is what I like to call The Dangerously Safe Investment:

Banks and building societies.

Isn't it strange how banks and building society savings accounts have fooled the people into false security?

The ultimate question here is then...

How's that working for you?

This is the question many people don't ask, but if they did, the answer would probably disappoint them. The returns a bank gives are so disappointingly low and the irony is that they themselves use the money people perceive to be a safe investment to loan out or use in other investment strategies that bring in so much more. How about we cut out this middle man and put our money to good use, and make much greater returns than the bank could ever make for us.

Are banks safe anymore?

Most of us used to assume that banks were the surest investment, but then the collapse of Lehman Brothers, leading to bankruptcy in 2008, ushered in a whole new era of banking. We have seen a number of banks collapse since, a number of high street UK banks on the brink of closing their doors forever only being saved by the UK government at the last minute. You only need to look at Greece and see what recently happened there with the money in people's accounts – could we ever have imagined that the government could dip into accounts and just take money, leaving people with only a fraction of their savings?

But not only that – banks rub salt into the wounds of their savings account customers.

Well, typically, in a savings account, the interest is low compared to other investments, which many people think is good.

However, if inflation is at say the target of 2%, and your interest payment is 2% per annum you are not really making any extra interest in the bank, and that is considering that the government is actually at a target of 2%. If inflation is higher than your interest rates, you may be losing money in real terms. But does the cost of living only increase by 2% per year? Utility bills, milk, bread, and fuel, all these necessities seem to be increasing by more than that 2%. So in fact you're losing money.

This proves that banks are most definitely not the best investment you can make, you can do better for sure.

Now that we are aware that banks are not safe or lucrative investments at all and that we really shouldn't view them as a safe investment, let us move on to the second traditional investment.

The second type of traditional investment is the stock and commodities market.

One major disadvantage of the stock market is that there is no stability. For example a stock that is doing relatively well over time would have gone into a serious negative position on 9/11 with the terrorist attack on the twin towers in America.

You simply cannot reliably predict what's going to happen with any particular company. One of the recent examples in history was Polly Peck International, a small British textile company which expanded rapidly in the 1980s and became a constituent of the FTSE 100 Index before collapsing in 1990 with debts of £1.3bn, eventually leading to the flight of its CEO, Asil Nadir to Northern Cyprus in 1993. The same can be said for many commodities; oil prices can fluctuate so drastically due to global political factors.

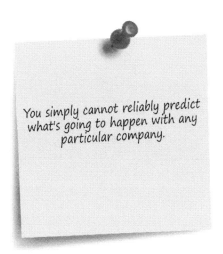

You simply cannot reliably predict what's going to happen with any particular company.

Food stocks can be at significant different values just depending on the weather! There are just too many uncontrollable factors.

Some would say it's the closest thing to gambling.

When we invest in the stock market and similar speculative investments, the returns look great. However, it's a gamble as you simply you don't know where you stand at any given point.

I am not saying you shouldn't invest in speculative investments. All I'm saying is be prepared to invest the amount of money you are willing to lose, because that is what most people do – lose their hard earned capital.

Market makers, stockbrokers and you.

There are a couple of points to be aware of. Have you noticed stockbrokers are always on hand to advise you of great investments, yet they never tend to invest themselves?

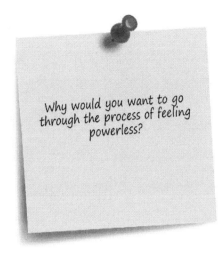

Why would you want to go through the process of feeling powerless?

Many years ago, I was invited to see what kind of work was carried out on a trading floor. After speaking to quite a few of the brokers there, it was clear to me that they did not want to invest due to the risk involved. However, when it comes to your money, they will happily invest it for you, and sell you all the dreams that buying a certain number of shares will get you. In reality, that is not how it works in the stock market. The salt in the wound for this investment is that you have no control over anything when it comes to this investment. Market makers decide the price when you buy and when you sell, they have total control over this. Why would you want to go through the process of feeling powerless?

So after looking at the facts, you may agree that you do not want to invest in the stock market.

The third traditional investment is property.

So what are the facts about property? The reason why property in the United Kingdom is such a great asset class is because there is solid historical evidence showing the trends and the cycles that occur. Property prices have been recorded for hundreds of years, and by analysing this data, it can be discovered that on average, every 10 years, house prices will increase by 100%.

The second reason why property is a great asset class is because it gives you capital appreciation and residual income at the same time. What other investment does that?

In the stock market, you will have to sell your shares to gain a profit (and that is if there is even a profit there) and if a company decides to pay dividends they can vary from year to year or cease at any time, and as we have already seen the same applies to savings accounts.

However, with property, your asset gains value, and there will always be a demand for property in the UK as we live on an island and there is a shortage of homes. Secondly, you receive income because not everyone can afford to purchase a property to live in, so they are happy to pay you to live in a property that you own.

Now we have looked at the facts of these investments, you can see that property is a great asset class to be investing in.

Namely, there are three key reasons why you should invest in property:

INSUFFICIENT PENSION

From my experience of mentoring hundreds of investors and working with clients in our property portfolio building company, my team and I have come to see that the primary reason you should invest in property is if you feel that you have an insufficient pension.

Many people who choose to invest in property do so

because they are concerned about their pension provision. They are afraid that they will not be able to live off of their poor performing pension.

Too many people work so hard their whole life, so they can finally retire and have a life of freedom and leisure. In reality, it does not work like that. They are led to a false sense of security.

SELLING TIME FOR MONEY

The second key reason is because many people are selling their time for money; however property is completely different to that. People have to go to work in order to be paid. Let's say for example, someone works eight hours a day, a typical 9-5 day. That person is only paid for their eight hours and they have to work eight hours. That is one third of their day that they have to sacrifice to be able to afford to maintain their current lifestyle. That is what I mean here by selling time for money. Property can release you from that.

NO TIME TO ENJOY LIFE

The third key reason to be investing in property is if you feel like you have no time to enjoy life. Property is a great investment if someone wants to have time to enjoy life. We all live busy lives, but the meaning of busy varies from person to person.

Property is a great investment if someone wants to have time to enjoy life.

Time is something that is very precious and we should cherish each moment.

Some people would class busy as having to work, then a post meeting after work, and then filing papers as busy, whereas others class busy as going on holiday, and arranging four activities a day to participate in. Time is something that is very precious and we should cherish each moment with the people who are a big part of our lives, whether those people are your friends, your children or your partner.

WHY DO I INVEST IN PROPERTY?

The reason I invest in property, and have done for the last two and a half decades, is because I truly believe property is the vehicle to a life of complete freedom and choice. The income from my properties means that I no longer have to worry about my lifestyle, pension, bills, or my children's future, as the property portfolio I have has secured all of that.

The reason I am still investing in property is because, as humans, we all have the need to grow. The more properties that are in my portfolio, the more income I have, and so the more people I can help in the world. What else would you do when you have an excess of money? More than what you need to live a life of leisure and comfort? You would begin to help other people.

WHO AM I?

My full name is Anoop Kumar Dovedi, and everyone knows me as Kam Dovedi. I am a professional property investor. The phrase "I am a professional property investor" is thrown around a lot, but what does it actually mean? I would consider a professional property investor as someone who is buying property on a regular monthly basis, has a wealth of knowledge and experience in their niche area, and is someone who has a solid team around them that allows them to achieve results efficiently.

Due to the knowledge and results gained through my property journey, I have been invited to speak in front of thousands of great people at events nationally, have had the opportunity to be interviewed by public figures in property, and have been asked to write articles in leading property magazines.

THE JOURNEY OF A LIFETIME

I have been a property investor since 1988, buying my first house at the tender age of 18, and have been investing in property for the last 25 years. As I sit here, writing this book for you at the Double Tree's Sky Lounge overlooking the rich heritage along the beautiful Thames river, I am laughing to myself as the time has definitely flown by.

I have built a multi-million pound portfolio, which brings in a monthly income that I could easily retire on. The reason I can sit here and write about how great property is as an investment, is because my property business is not the only business I have.

Although I have other six and seven figure businesses ranging from import/export, wholesaling, retailing, and ecommerce, property is definitely the most rewarding and fun, and the profits that are made by the other companies are reinvested to grow the property portfolio. This is because the long term growth property gives you is fantastic.

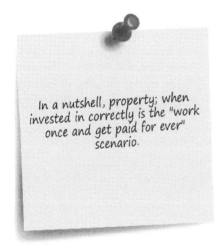

In a nutshell, property; when invested in correctly is the "work once and get paid for ever" scenario.

In a nutshell, property, when invested in correctly, is a "work once and get paid for ever" scenario. The knowledge and experience gained from the years of investing, building valuable relationships with key people, building a strong team to systemise processes, has allowed me to do many things that I truly love. First, it has allowed me to become the founder of Premier Portfolio Builder, a property portfolio building company where people are able to leverage us to achieve outstanding results without having to invest any of their own time, effort or knowledge.

Also, it has allowed me to create a monthly event, The Premier Property Networking Club, where I can invite my friends to deliver keynote seminars to share their knowledge with people, as they all have six, seven or eight figure property businesses.

Thirdly it has allowed me to become a public speaker and mentor. I am so grateful to have shared my knowledge with hundreds of investors across the UK; it is a truly humbling experience.

But it wasn't always like that. And I don't say any of this to impress you, I just mention these facts about me because I believe it is important for you to know whose book you are reading. I genuinely hope you find this book valuable, beneficial and can benefit from the knowledge I share with you.

But like I said, it wasn't always like that.

It was definitely not easy, and in order to show you the point in my life where everything changed we have to go back to 1969, when my mother and father came over from India...

My mother was a simple village girl, surviving day-to-day life by scraping the bare necessities together, and sometimes having to even live without them. Contrastingly, my father was a very well educated man, with an almost regal aura, however he had a serious alcohol problem.

As I was growing up as a child, I saw my mother struggle to provide for us. She had a job as a seamstress, where she would work the best part of 16 hours a day to put food on the table. In the winter months, I saw how she would walk a mile in the bitter cold, just to avoid paying the bus fare, as there was not enough in our 'pot' for that. At the age of 11 I understood what was going on, and I vowed that I would take my mother out of this. So I got my first job at this age as a paper round boy. Rain, sleet, or snow, I would be delivering papers at 6 a.m. each morning before I went to school.

As I got older, I moved from job to job, and there was one job where the path I was on changed. At the age of 16 I was working at one of the biggest independent department stores in the clothing sector. If you are from London then you probably remember Sammy and Saleem's department store in east London. From time to time, Sammy the department store owner would have brief conversations with me. The fact that that I was only 16 and a man who was a multi-millionaire would come and speak to me was just amazing. He was such a wise and inspirational man. He said two things that would prove to be so true.

The first was "Everyone who works in this clothing department of my store goes on to make a career in the clothing business, and many become extremely successful in business. All the big wholesalers you see on commercial road London E1, they started here. You are here, and you will forever be in this game". As I sat and heard him say that, I thought *Yeah right, I don't want to be doing this forever.* When I read it back, it sounds like a curse, but little did I know he was completely right. I look back and laugh now as my other business is the leader in a niche clothing sector, which I never would have believed then, but I guess Sammy knew exactly what he was talking about.

The second was "Boy, do you want to be working your whole life?" I said no. He said, "Do you know what this is?", and I said a business, as I genuinely thought that was the correct answer. He said "What this is, is my ticket to freedom". He then showed me how he was putting the profits he was making from his department store into property. He showed me how property worked, and how he would be paid continuously. He said in other markets, like in retail, things change too quickly. But with property, it takes a longer period of time, so you can plan and prepare. Sammy had introduced me to a completely new world at the age of 16 that I hadn't even known existed. So I listened, and for the next two years, I was saving my money in order to buy a house.

So when I turned 18 I did what Sammy told me, and invested in my first property. The results I achieved from this one house then seemed to be fantastic, but if I did what I did then now, I would most definitely not call it fantastic.

Of course it was my first property, and as I went on I learned more, and gathered momentum. It was just a wild decision at the age of 18, and at that age you feel invincible. So now with this even greater feeling of invincibility, I bought another, and another, and another, and the ball was rolling and I was gaining momentum.

Then, when I turned 21, I tried to explain to my bank manager what I was doing, and this was before the times of buy to let.

Then, when I turned 21, I tried to explain to my bank manager what I was doing, and this was before the times of buy to let.

Do you know what he said to me? He said "Oh no, that is not something we would lend on as it is too risky". This burst my bubble of enthusiasm.

Then a surveyor said something similar to me. I began to doubt myself, as what I thought I had here was something great, and someone with letters after their name didn't agree. These men were professionals in my eyes, and because of that, I felt I should listen to them and always take their advice. Then, my friends and family began saying similar things to me, and because I knew they truly cared for me, I listened and I felt like everyone was against the idea of property.

So what do you do? Being young and naive I took a back seat, and instead of buying at least 3-10 properties a month like I do now, I slowed down, and my focus changed to building another business. Property, the vehicle that was truly going to help me reach freedom, had slowed down.

At the back of my mind, there was a little voice saying *property is good, do it, invest, invest*. So I listened, and I began educating myself. To date, I have paid well over several hundreds of thousands of pounds for my education. Some of my mentors I have now, I pay five and even six figures to learn the new cutting edge techniques, ideas and systems to streamline the businesses we have now even further.

Back then, even though I was continuously educating myself, I was not taking action to my maximum potential. Maybe you have experienced that, where you can be doing a lot better, but the people around you are pulling you back.

Then one day everything changed.

17th February 2008.

It was three in the afternoon. A huge grey cloud had cast a shadow over London, and hadn't given any sign of surrendering for three days. Rain was falling so heavily, like nothing I had seen before, and all I could see and hear as I looked out my living room window was the rain smashing angrily against the window pane. In the reflection, I saw something that you would never ever want to see. I saw all of my credit card statements laid across the patched up carpet floor. At that point in my life, I was £157,000 in debt because I had 'pumped' money into a business where the market had rapidly declined over the last six months, and I didn't know what to do, who to turn to or where to go.

I felt the energy drain from my body, as I sat there, holding my head in my hands. I couldn't think, my mind was filled to the brink with overwhelming interest charges and the extortionate APRs I was paying.

As I sat there with my head in my hands, there was a knock at the door. There was something so strange about the knock, the sound echoed down my corridor as if with a negative wave penetrating through my body. As I opened the door, what looked like a complete stranger was in fact my mum. She walked past me, as if I was a stranger, into the dining room. I smelled something, like those hand sanitisers you get in hospitals.

She sat down and brushed the rain off her face. My mum, warm, bubbly, beautiful and always smiling, was definitely not the woman in front of me now. Her eyes were red and bloodshot, the skin under her eyes was inflamed, she had been crying. Her face was pale, and I could see the blue-green veins in her cheeks. It looked like all her energy had been sucked out of her. She looked so...powerless, and this was not like my mum at all. As she opened her mouth to speak, she stopped, looked down and pursed her lips. She then looked up at me. She put her hand on my hand, and she felt so cold – ice cold – and for the first time, I felt the wrinkles in her skin. As her mouth opened she said "I didn't want you to worry", and at that point I sunk.

I had this disgusting feeling in my gut. You know that feeling when you are about to be sick? The blood rushed to my head, and my ears began ringing. My eyes were fixated on my mum, listening to every uneasy breath. Then she said, "I have been going to the doctors, and I have had some tests done". She took a breath, lifted her head, and looked at me straight in my eyes and she said "I have....."

She said that word. That terrible, hated six-letter word that so many of our lives have been touched by. That word we want to chew up and spit out, that word that makes us all so angry, that word that has crushed relationships, and ruined lives.

She said, "I have cancer".

As she said these words, she completely broke down. I went completely blank. I could not believe what I was being told.

So I lifted her head up, and wiped the tears from her face, and just hugged her like I had never done before. While I held the most important woman in my life, all I could think was, here was a woman, who had sacrificed so much for me, and I could not have even been a success for her. I could not have even been the best I could have been for her. What would I do? Where would I go? Who could I turn to? How could I get her out of this? So I did all that I could do. I shouted, at the top of my voice, from within: Please make her better, to the universe, to God, to my angel, I begged and pleaded to make her better, and in return I promised so many outrageous things, that I would help people, give hope to those who have no hope, so many outrageous promises, that I had no idea how I would fulfil.

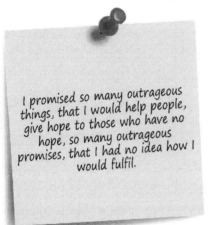

I promised so many outrageous things, that I would help people, give hope to those who have no hope, so many outrageous promises, that I had no idea how I would fulfil.

So my mum started her treatment. It wasn't easy for her, it was a lengthy process, but she responded better than the doctors had imagined. She gradually showed signs of recovery over time, and I began to see the colour in her cheeks again, and the sparkle in her hazelnut brown eyes. She was back to chatting with her friends, making new friends in an instant, rushing around, helping everyone around her, whether they needed help or not and annoyingly treating me like I was a five-year-old. She was back.

Now what? I had made all of these promises, how would I fulfil them? Where would I start? The answer stared me right in the face, the same answer Sammy had given me at the age of 16. Property.

So my accelerated journey in property began, and through property, I began to help people, began to give hope to those who have none, and truly began to set people free financially.

So let's fast forward to today. My mum lives in one of my properties, a £1.1 million house that I own.

She has nothing to worry about. She lives a life of freedom, and what funds her pension is my property portfolio. The reason she is free is because she doesn't have to think about her bills, or funding her lifestyle, she doesn't have to work today, she doesn't have to think she can't buy that extra little luxury or it is too expensive.

She need not worry about any of these things. I am truly grateful for property and what it has done for me and my family, and I believe in a world of true freedom, a world where we no longer sacrifice our time for money, a world where we are able to fulfil our passions and potential to the maximum.

Today, I am the founder of Premier Portfolio Builder, one of the fastest-growing property portfolio building companies in the south east of England, which allows me to fulfil my purpose and what I believe.

Today I am the founder The Premier Property Networking Club, where we reach out to as many people as possible to share with them why property is such an amazing vehicle.

Today, I am free.

And do you know what the beauty is? The more people I can help, through all the different businesses, the bigger my pot grows, which means I can help even more people, and it will keep growing. So why did I even share my story with you?

The first reason is because I believe you are someone who

takes action, someone who goes against the grain and someone who wants to take control of their own destiny. I shared my story because I want you to find your purpose without there having to be a life changing event.

Why wait for something like that to happen to realise you are capable of great things? So whether your purpose is to help people, to spend quality time you have with your children and partner, or to leave a legacy, it's simple; find your purpose and you will begin on your accelerated journey of success, to become even more successful than you are today.

When someone has been in business for a long time like me, the results you achieve are what you are known for. I am grateful that I have been able to help people along my journey, and I am truly blessed for the opportunities I receive. In any business, your reputation precedes you, and this is the one of the most important factors which will allow you to become successful.

Sukhi Wahiwala (SukhiWahiwala.com) Business Coach of the Year Award winner, says...

"I have known Kam for a number of years and have got to know Kam very well through working with him on various projects across his many successful businesses.

He is a very competent professional property investor, with clear tried and tested strategies.

What many people do not know about Kam is his bigger mission, and his deep down "why" for why he does what he does. This bigger mission has taken him from strength to strength, accelerating not only his own success, but the success of people he is able to help.

Kam has this ability that only a handful of us have, where he is able to assess the needs of others, and deliver real solutions for them, day in and day out with a combined jovial and focused nature.

As an established business mentor with experience of helping 1000s to success, I have recognised Kam is a real action taker, who remembers where he has come from, and I have found him to be a very humble, sincere, and genuine person.

Onwards & upwards!"

Juspal Nagra Senior mortgage broker at Trafalgar Square Financial Planning Consultants says... "Kam has assisted a number of my clients and always provided a fast and efficient service. His honesty, integrity and his welcoming smile go a long way to provide clients with the comfort required. He always has the client's interest at heart"

Daniel Wagner CEO of Expert Success and 7 Figure Business Man, says... "I first noticed Kam at one of our intensive training days. I only learned later on that Kam was a very experienced and successful property investor. Kam has successfully refined a hands free model for busy professionals. One of the interesting aspects of Kam's expert positioning is his unconscious competence and natural humility. A high achiever with a great work ethic, he always manages a lot of different projects, not giving himself the credit that he is due".

Arsh Ellahi LHA specialist says... *"There's not many people that I trust in property, but Kam's someone who I trust completely. Very knowledgeable and successful yet down to earth person."*

Georg Alscher CEO of European Division at ePrime Global, says... *"I have got to know Kam through a dear friend. If you ask me to sum up his character in short, I'd say he is an inspirational & focus-driven property investment manager. If you need a knowledgeable, reliable person in property investment, get in touch with Kam. My full recommendation!"*

Jim Campbell says... *"My dealings with Kam have proved him to be a highly knowledgeable individual in property development. His ability to remain level-headed and effective in situations others would find stressful means that I would highly recommend Kam to any potential business partner."*

Ed Hackett-Jones (Director) says... *"I have a great deal of respect for Kam. Kam has an ability to focus right in on the crux of an issue and come up with the most appropriate solution. I can say that if I were looking for help in building my property portfolio or for some property mentorship, I would definitely work with Kam, and I would willingly suggest others do too."*

Sudeshna Choudhury Credit control manager at Millards Cleaning Services Ltd., says... *"Kam is a very hard working and smart entrepreneur who really cares about his clients and is dedicated to giving them the best possible service. He is extremely knowledgeable and experienced in creative property deals as an expert in his field, but also* *generous about sharing his expertise with others. I would recommend him as a very reliable person and will deliver whatever he promises."*

Derek Archibald Owner of Creative Home Solutions, says... *"Kam is a very experienced and trustworthy property investor and a genuine guy who goes out of his way to help others and can be relied upon to give excellent results".*

Tommy Franzen Dancer/choreographer/sports massage therapist/property investor/NLP & hypnotherapy practitioner, says... *"Kam has provided me excellent service and skill. Brought me a great deal, gave me access to his power team to make the purchase quick and smooth, instructed his refurb team, let it out quickly and is now managing my property. Highly recommended!"*

Nicki Pakunwanich Professional property investor, says... *"Kam is an extremely innovative and experienced property investor – with an extensive property portfolio worth several million pounds, and several years of property experience. Not only is he attaining high yields from his latest, cutting-edge "hands free" solution generating large income for his clients and himself, but also from his personal property development portfolio which alone is worth millions. Kam's one to one mentoring service is an absolutely unmissable service. Highly recommended."*

Lyubka Mihailova Creative property problem solver, says... *"Kam is a trustworthy property professional, who knows what he is doing and, importantly, would not mislead people. He possesses steady skills and is certainly* *the go-to person if you want to build a low risk portfolio relatively quickly."*

Ann Boone, MBA, Founder and trustee at Relief from Pain Charity, says..."*Kam is someone with an amazing energy, having experience in successfully running various different types of businesses. He is someone who is interested in knowing you a bit better first, so he understands what your requirements are and how he can help you in finding the right solutions for you. He is very well connected and respected amongst peers and will recommend any one of them if their solution suits you better. He is credible, honest and delivers. I would highly recommend Kam for his property service. Connect with him today.* "

Julie Smith Director, Foot Motion Ltd., says... *"Kam is a genuine helpful person who looks at your needs when helping to build a property portfolio. He will give his honest opinion in a non-biased fashion, always considering what is right for the client."*

Jim Haliburton HMO Daddy, says..."*This young man has done great things for himself, and is doing great things for other people, get to know him."*

HOW CAN INVESTING IN PROPERTY TRULY HELP YOU?

The question then is, why should you be investing in property? What challenges does it actually solve?

BOOST YOUR RETIREMENT INCOME

The first challenge property solves is an insufficient pension. Property investing is not a get rich quick scheme.

Property investing is about becoming extremely wealthy over time, and is a long term and sustainable source of income.

We now live in a world where, because of technological and medical advancements, the aging population is increasing, and the birth rate is decreasing. This means there are less people working, which means pension pots are shrinking, and the retirement age barrier is rising – that's why you now need to take control of your own pension.

Imagine having control of your own pension – a pension that allows you to live a comfortable life and maintain your lifestyle after you have retired. Well, that is the pension property can give you.

AVOID SELLING TIME FOR MONEY

Are you selling your time for money? Are you stuck in a job that you no longer love because circumstances have changed? Do you find yourself working harder than ever for little reward?

This is what I mean by selling your time for money. In essence that is what a job is, you spend nine hours each day of your life at work (or whatever that number is for you), working incredibly hard to have the money to do what you love, but there is a lot of time lost in the process.

This time could be spent with your loved ones, doing hobbies you love to do, and giving you time to make an even bigger difference to people's lives if that is what you choose to do.

The myth about having a job is that it is secure, but did you know that during the recession in the UK, according to The Telegraph article written on 24 Jan 2010, 1.3 million people lost their jobs? Are jobs really safe?

I recently went to visit the Coca Cola factory with my daughter. I was astonished to discover that in the whole factory there were only two hundred people working there. The rest of the workers had been replaced by machines, which are more efficient, and more cost effective. How would that feel, to be replaced by a machine? Why am I sharing this with you? I am sharing this with you because I believe that we live in a world where you must take control of your own destiny.

What property allows you to have is a safe secure and residual income, which means you can then choose when you want to work, should you even want to work. This residual income gives you time and choices that truly allow you to live your life your way.

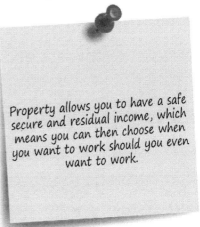

Property allows you to have a safe secure and residual income, which means you can then choose when you want to work should you even want to work.

CREATE MORE TIME TO ENJOY YOUR LIFE

Right now, ask yourself this question: "Am I in a position to enjoy life?" Out of the hundreds of people I have worked with, many had no time to enjoy life before they got into property because they were always preoccupied with finances.

Like me, you may have heard a parent say to their child "I don't have time for that", or "I'm too busy so I can't come today". The children of today are being neglected because everyone who is in a job is being overworked to receive some income, to survive.

Property can be your safety net, and by leveraging and using this asset class, you too can enjoy your life. Property gives you time, and this time can be used to enjoy your life to the fullest. A life of freedom comes after we secure our finances for the long term, so we need not worry about that part of life, because we know that residual income will be there month after month, after month.

One of the people I have worked with is Caroline Butson. Caroline is someone who I have got to know very well since working with her. Before we started working together, she was very risk averse and because of all the apparent "experts" in the market place, she was afraid to take action.

However, because I could show her real projects we were doing, provide her real testimonials and because of what people would say about me she began to trust me. I was able to answer any questions she had, and would always act in her best interest, because knowing I have done something of value for someone else makes me feel good.

So what did she achieve? Caroline was able to build a property portfolio without using any of her time and effort, because that is the service that my company offers. She was able to leverage my teams, my knowledge and my experience, and because everything was done for her, from sourcing through to refurbishment and then the ongoing letting and management, Caroline achieved fantastic accelerated results. From the testimonials she has provided for us, she has said that if she had tried to do it herself it would have taken at least three times longer, plus she would have made many mistakes along the way. The reason we can provide results with no mistakes and maximum time saving is because of the formula we have nurtured, refined and grown over the last 25 years.

KEY LEARNINGS

1. Property is an asset class that increases in value over time.

2. Property investing provides a residual income.

3. Income from property is passive.

4. By investing in property, you no longer trade your time for money.

5. Property is for the medium to long term.

6. Property investing is not a get rich quick scheme.

7. Property value fluctuations are less compared to other investments.

8. Property investing increases your pension pot.

9. Property investing helps tackle inflation.

10. Know your reason why you want to invest in property, as this is when the method to achieve success in property becomes much easier.

CHAPTER 2

WHAT YOU NEED TO KNOW TO BE A SUCCESSFUL PROPERTY INVESTOR

In order to become a successful property investor, there are certain areas in which you must have knowledge and experience, to make your property investing journey much easier. In this chapter, I will be touching upon the different areas you must have knowledge in, so that you can be extremely successful in property.

EFFECTIVE STRATEGY

The first part to becoming a successful property investor is through knowing an effective strategy and then being able to implement it.

A strategy can only be effective once you have implemented it; otherwise the strategy is just concept.

A strategy can only be effective once you have implemented it; otherwise the strategy is just a concept.

This is why I can share with you what I have found to be most effective, for both myself and the people I have worked with. In my eyes, an effective strategy is one where the risk is low, and the reward is high and continuous. Therefore, there are three main strategies that are used in property.

BUY AND SELL

The first of the three strategies is to buy and sell, or as our American friends call it, "flipping". This strategy is where you buy a property, look to add value and then would ideally like to sell the property for a profit. Like any strategy, it has its advantages and disadvantages. The main advantage of buying and then selling a property is that there is a potential for a profit to be made if done correctly.

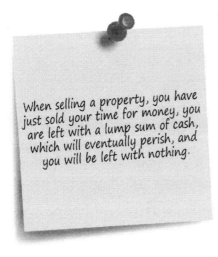

When selling a property, you have just sold your time for money, you are left with a lump sum of cash, which will eventually perish, and you will be left with nothing.

The disadvantages for this strategy do outweigh the advantages. For example, when selling a property, you have just sold your time for money, you are left with a lump sum of cash, which will eventually perish, and you will be left with nothing. This means that you will have to go and work again, to find a property and then once again to sell it for a profit. This strategy is not passive.

The second disadvantage of the buy and sell strategy is the costs involved.

For example, generally from the properties I have bought and sold and the projects I have joint ventured on with others, the costs are high. This is because first of all we generally have to buy above stamp duty; therefore we pay a tax on the purchase.

Then the capital expenditure increases even further when you have to complete a refurbishment to the best specification so that someone will be attracted towards buying your property. Then you have the sale fees and solicitors' costs to consider. And if that wasn't enough, you also have to pay capital gains tax on any profit made.

After all that, if you have a lot of experience, teams, and resources, you may be left with a profit.

I have seen too many investors *think* they have made a profit during a buy and sell, but once they look at the time they have put in and all of the exit costs the profit may actually be a loss. Something you may want to think about.

The third disadvantage is that the buy and sell strategy is not long term. By buying and selling an asset like property, you are not appreciating the immense power it has if it is kept over time.

Once a property has been sold, you no longer receive residual passive income from it. You no longer receive the capital appreciation from it. This ultimately means you are not securing your income or financial future.

This shows how the buy and sell strategy is a short term fix. Of course, done correctly, you may generate some cash, which will not last forever. I believe in the concept of working once and being paid forever; this allows you to create time, which is why the buy and sell strategy is not something that I focus on as the ultimate end goal.

CREATIVE STRATEGIES

Creative strategies – they are known as creative for a reason.

These strategies have not been established, tried, tested or proven to work over a long period of time, but let's look at the advantages of creative strategies. There are currently three types of creative strategies: rent to rent, lease options and HMOs, and I will be sharing with you the advantages and disadvantages of each below.

Firstly, let's look at the rent to rent strategy. So what actually is rent to rent? It is where landlords are offered a guaranteed rent. You find tenants to live in the property and manage the property. You make your profit on the difference between the rent you pay to the owner and the rent you get paid by your tenants minus the costs.

The main advantage of rent to rent is that it can be made in to a great business if done correctly with little capital input, as you do not need to own the property in order to receive cash flow from it. However, in the rent to rent case, the negatives do outweigh the positives.

The first disadvantage is that you are not in control, as the property is not yours. The landlord can ask for the property back at any time, and through a buy and sell, the landlord may even change so your agreement may no longer be valid with the new landlord, therefore you are too dependent on the current landlord.

The second disadvantage is that the property is not yours. This means that you will lose any future potential capital growth, as the property is not yours. You will also not be the long term owner, so you are not involved in the decisions made about the property.

The third disadvantage is the responsibility around the rent to rent strategy.

Many people think this strategy is very easy, but in essence what you are really doing is creating a letting agency. The tenants that are in the property are your responsibility; if one leaves, it is your job to find another, and if one ruins the property, it is your responsibility to clean up their mess.

To add to that point, you have guaranteed the landlord a certain rent, which you must pay them each month, regardless of your circumstances, and in some cases you might inadvertently be causing the owner to commit mortgage fraud, because any lending on the property usually will not allow the owner to sublet, and this is what you are doing.

The second creative strategy is the lease options strategy, which again is not the traditional method of buying property. So what actually is a lease option? A lease option is an agreement that gives a renter the option to purchase a property during or at the end of the rental period. As long as the **lease option** period is in effect, the landlord/seller may not offer the property for sale to anyone else in the market. To be completely honest with you, I only know a handful of people who this strategy has worked for, and in my eyes, I can only see negatives with this strategy.

First of all you are very reliant on the mortgagee not defaulting, or going bankrupt. Secondly, it's not really a tried and tested market; no one really knows what will happen on the exit of a long term option, which may be 25 years in reality and many option deals have not reached their exit date, so what if markets and circumstances change in that 25 year period? You are stuck in a contract until the exit date and it is really an ambiguous concept.

The third and final creative strategy I will mention is the Houses in Multiple Occupation (HMO) strategy. So what is a HMO? A HMO refers to residential properties where 'common areas' exist and are shared by more than one household. Common areas may be bathrooms and kitchens, but may also be just stairwells or landings. HMOs may be divided up into self-contained flats, bed-sitting rooms or simple lodgings.

Like the other creative strategies, HMOs have their advantages and disadvantages. The advantage is that, on paper, it looks like you will receive a lot more income compared to other strategies. The advocates of HMOs allegedly boast a 20% plus return. The figures on paper are a HMOs biggest advantage.

However what people don't tend to realise is that in reality HMOs do not really work. There is a saying that my multi-millionaire mentors have taught me: "Turnover is vanity, profit is sanity", so even though the turnover looks appealing, the profit is not so appealing.

The first disadvantage of a HMO is the capital you have to use in order to even produce a gross income from the property. To be able to buy, refurbish and provide furnishings for the property, costs a lot more. Usually for what it costs, with a mortgage, you are able to buy an additional 'single let' family home property with one tenancy for the whole property.

The second disadvantage is the management of HMOs. Many managing agents will either not take on HMOs as they know the work involved, or an agent will take on the HMO and then hand it back to you six months later because they have discovered the intense work involved in being able to manage and maintain the income from a HMO.

This disadvantage of management can be strengthened further through the type of tenant profile you have in the property. For example, if you have a professional in your property, do you really think they will be in your HMO property for long?

And if you have a tenant on benefits in your HMO, imagine all the monetary grief and aggravation you might face in trying to manage the property.

What happens if they stop receiving benefits that will cover your costs? The fact of the matter is, your voids, and time lost, will destroy the chances of you even making any profits from your HMO, so it is not a strategy I recommend for someone, especially someone who is starting their journey into property or looking for a strong, sustainable strategy to boost their income and increase their income for the long term.

The third disadvantage is the cost involved in actually maintaining your HMO. The electric, gas and other energy bills are to be paid by the landlord, and council tax is also to be paid by the landlord. Do you really think your tenant cares about their landlord? Do you think they will turn off their lights when they are not in the room? Do you think they will close their window while they have the heating on? The answer is no. This is because it is not their home, they are just living there and they know that the energy bills are inclusive of their agreement with you. The amount of energy a HMO uses is not to be sniffed at; the energy costs will drain your profits, and drag them into a loss.

The last disadvantage I will mention is one that I have learnt from speaking to mortgage brokers. The owner of a HMO in most cases actually is committing mortgage fraud if they have not taken a specialist mortgage and have taken out a mortgage to rent to one household and then rent to separate tenants. Many people think that a HMO is a buy to let, so that is the mortgage they go for, and without even knowing, they are committing mortgage fraud, for which the penalties are very strict. So once again, HMOs are not something I would recommend purely because of the costs, time, effort and legal implications involved.

BUY TO LET

The third and final strategy is the buy to let strategy, and what I am sharing with you here is the single let strategy, which means the property is let out as one whole unit, usually to a family.

This is the strategy that I truly believe in, as it is one I have implemented, implement now, and will always implement due to all of the advantages and rewards this strategy provides.

So what actually is a buy to let/single let? It is where you purchase a property with the specific intention to then let the property out. This strategy has made me a great amount of wealth, and that wealth will increase and accelerate over time. I will be discussing the advantage and disadvantage of the single let strategy, so let's start with the disadvantage.

The main disadvantage of a single let is that you must find the correct investment area before you purchase your property.

It is important that you have a complete economical process in place to achieve a long term rental income for each property, and be able to remove risk from all aspects of the process, from the purchase to refurbishment and with the ongoing lettings and management. In London, the single let concept in most cases doesn't work, as the yield is too low compared to the price you are paying.

Alternatively, if you are investing in the north of the country you receive a good yield, but you lose the capital growth which investing in or near London will get you. However, where I invest, and where my company Premier Portfolio Builder invests for our clients, we receive both the potential growth and the good yield at the same time. So in order to find this area, it may take you time. Luckily, out of good fortune, when I set up my first business and bought my first set of investment properties by the age of 23, it was in the same area I invest in now, so through sheer luck, I was in the right place before I even knew it.

However I would recommend first finding the correct area where all the investment figures work, and then invest.

Now, to the advantages.

The first advantage is that with a single let property, the management is easier, as it is just a single family in there, so a good letting agent would be able to manage the property for you without any hassle, and if you are organised and have systems in place like me, you or your company you establish may be able to manage the property for you.

The second advantage is that you own the property so you will receive all of the capital growth and income from the property, which will increase over time.

The next advantage is that you will be able to create time, and this all goes back to the goose and the golden egg fable. If you have a goose that is laying you a golden egg, month after month, why would you want to kill the goose? The single let strategy keeps your goose alive, and you receive a residual income from it. Therefore, you are working once, and being rewarded forever.

Another advantage is that the capital expenditure will be lower compared to other strategies. In a buy and sell and HMO strategy, you have to make everything perfect, spending large amounts of money on unnecessary items, whereas with a single let, you leave it unfurnished, and upgrade the property to a certain specification so that it is appealing to the rental market, not the buy to sell market, and there is a clear distinction between the two. As well as capital expenditure costs, the long term costs are minimal. This is because in a single let, the occupant pays the council tax and energy bills, so your profits are not drained, whereas in a HMO, you would normally pay these.

Another advantage of the single let strategy is that it is

tried and tested; there is a method behind it, and many case studies.

For example, we have a model for the single let strategy at Premier Portfolio Builder, and here is what one of our clients Emily Cusack had to say about it "I met The Premier Portfolio Builder team at a property show, and they showed me their hands free investing model. At that point I thought to myself I like the sound of that! It was really easy because I didn't have to do anything; all I had to do was sign the dotted line with the solicitors, and now I get cash flow from a property I own every month".

To add to the idea of the tried tested and proven model, the single let strategy is a low risk strategy. There are not huge costs involved – if property prices slightly dip, you are still making residual income, so it reduces any risk you may have.

The single let strategy is a low risk strategy.

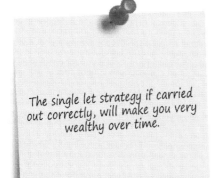

The single let strategy if carried out correctly, will make you very wealthy over time.

The last advantage of the single let strategy is that, if done correctly, it will make you very wealthy over time. The cash flow will increase as your portfolio increases, and if you are investing in a potential high growth area like me, the speed at which your portfolio is built can be accelerated. Before you know it, you will have a large cash flow amount, great enough to support or replace your income, and something that you can retire on.

WINNING TEAM

So now that we have established that the single let strategy is a fantastic strategy to implement in property, you will need a winning team. This is so important in order to put this strategy into practice effectively and in order to become a successful property investor.

A winning team is one that is built up over time, especially if you want the team to work together like clockwork. A team is where each person plays an important role in the process, and each individual needs to be equally as good as the next person in the process. For example, in football, each player must be as good as the next and they must gel together in order to win games. If there is just one star player, results will vary, and you will rely too heavily on that person, so it is crucial you build up a strong team.

Make sure you have a winning Team.

Likewise, in property, you want to make sure that you have multiple people in each position of your winning team, so that you are not too reliant on one person, because if that person leaves, or changes profession, you are left with a hole in your process.

In this part of the chapter, I will be sharing with you who you need in your team in order to make your single let strategy property journey a success.

PROFESSIONAL ADVISERS AND CONSULTANTS

Before you purchase a property, there are three professionals you must be working with in order to make the acquisition process a success.

The first professional you need in your team in order to become a successful property investor is an estate agent. An estate agent in the property world can be seen to be like a consultant, even though officially they may not be one.

The reason you need an agent on your team is because they are the people who will be able to offer you the correct properties so that you can implement your strategy. I work very closely with the estate agents in the areas in which my clients and I invest. Over many years I have been building relationships with these estate agents.

The fact that we are undertaking 3-10 property transactions each month helps to keep them on my team. The type of agent you are looking for is one who is organised, gets the job done, and is willing to go further than what is necessary in order to provide the best possible service that they possibly can.

What the agent is looking for from you is ease and reliability. They need to know that when you put an offer in for a property, you can definitely purchase the property, and I have many investors fall down here. They put in an offer, and when it comes to purchase they do not have the funds available, haven't been qualified to obtain a mortgage or simply aren't correctly organised to proceed quickly.

This amateur investor will 'pull out' of an agreed deal, or renegotiate after they have agreed a price which is unacceptable to an estate agent.

As soon as you break that trust between you and the agent, it is very difficult to rebuild it. So when working with an estate agent, make sure you are truthful, follow through with what is agreed and keep to your word, and this will show the estate agent you are a serious property investor.

Also, you want to make sure your attitude and approach when visiting the agent is in the right frame. The average Joe walks in to the estate agency and, knowing they have cash to invest in a property, throws down the proof of funds, and will assume the estate agent has to provide the correct property for them because they are cash rich, or have enough funds to invest in property.

If you take average Joe's approach, you will never be given a correct investment property to purchase. It is important to realise there are many investors with cash who want to invest in property. It really is about building a relationship with the agent, and yes this can mean they will test you. You may have to purchase a number of properties, before they consider you a serious investor and then start to offer you properties only their best investors ever get to purchase.

So now to the 'real' professional advisers.

There are two different professionals you need in order to

become a successful property investor, a mortgage broker and a solicitor. I am now at a point where I work with multiple mortgage brokers (one of which speaks at our monthly event, The Premier Property Networking Club) and multiple solicitors who are really fantastic at what they do: fast, reliable and efficient.

I work with mortgage brokers and solicitors very closely on a daily basis, however when you are starting, you need to build strong relationships first... and then scale. So let's look at why you need a mortgage broker and what criteria your mortgage broker should tick in order to be considered as "good".

The reason you have a mortgage broker is because they are able to show you products from different lenders, and they are able to advise you on what your best options are. The average Joe would walk into their local bank and apply for a mortgage, not having considered their options or the long term implications.

The average Joe may have thought about going to a mortgage broker, but the fact the mortgage broker is charging for their service they offer may have put them off and the charges can vary considerably.

What the average Joe does not know is that finding the correct broker will involve a small cost and is irrelevant, as the product they will find for you will save you thousands of pounds over time. The only caveat is you need to be sure the mortgage broker is an expert in their field, not just have the qualifications to be accepted as a mortgage broker, and we will now discuss this.

So now that we know why we must have a mortgage

broker in our team, what criteria must your mortgage broker have to be considered as a "good mortgage broker"? I have outlined some criteria for you below:

1. How quickly do they respond? If you call them do they answer and reply back very quickly? Do they reply to your messages and emails?

    This allows you to get a feel for how organised the mortgage broker is, and is an under the radar way of discovering that. Testing their speed, and how quickly they respond now, will be the same as how quickly they will respond in the future.

2. Are they "whole of market"? This is an important criterion as if they have access to the whole market of mortgage products, it means they can see and provide more products than the average broker.

    If a whole of market mortgage broker finds a product for you, that saves you 0.5% annualised interest for your mortgage. Over time this may actually equate to thousands of pounds, so the only way a mortgage broker can have checked the entire market, is if they are whole of market.

3. Are their values aligned with yours? Because if they are, you will enjoy working with them, everything will seem that much easier, and you will benefit from the best results.

4. Are you just a number? Or are you a person? This is an important one. No one wants to be a figure on a spreadsheet; everyone wants to be treated like a person. Our mortgage brokers do that, and the

reason for that is we have the same values, we are personable.

5. Do they think long term? Property is not about making a quick 'buck' and then leaving. It is about building serious long term wealth, and having a mortgage broker who thinks like that is amazing. This is because, ultimately, it will show that they too are in this for the long term, and their reputation is important.

Those five questions above are the main questions to think about when working with a mortgage broker.

The third professional you need is a solicitor. A great solicitor like the solicitors we have, make the acquisition a simple, smooth and secure process.

A good solicitor is one who not only knows exactly what they are doing, but is someone that you can work with long term.

If there is friction between you and the solicitor, you can almost guarantee that the acquisition process will be delayed, which means that you may lose the property you were just about to purchase. So once again, just like the mortgage broker, what should you be looking for in a "good" solicitor?

1. Have they got an existing client base for conveyancing? Conveyancing is the transfer of the legal title of a property from one person to another. The reason for this is because, in a solicitor's office, there needs to be a structure and everything needs to be organised so that you can achieve the best results.

So if there is an existing client base, their model has been tried tested and proven, which means that they are a solicitor that you should consider. You do not want to go to a solicitor who is very new, as they will not have the correct amount of experience to help you if certain aspects of the property process become challenging.

2. Are they old school? We are not looking for solicitors who are simply just compliant with what needs to be done. We are looking for solicitors that will go the extra mile. What I mean by this is that are they a solicitor who will check everything down to the last little detail. A solicitor like this will get you the best long term results, and will not shortcut the process. They will check for the most unlikely of things, to make sure that they will not affect you. They will read the contracts thoroughly and highlight anything that may seem unusual. You want a solicitor like that, because as we have established, the single let strategy is a long term strategy.

We are looking for solicitors that will go the extra mile. What I mean by this is that are they a solicitor who check everything down to the last little detail.

3. How quickly do they communicate? If you call them do they reply very quickly? Do they reply to your messages and emails? Is there a team in the office? It is important there is, because what do you do if your solicitor is on holiday or unwell while your purchase

is going through? A team of solicitors means your purchase can still be dealt with correctly.

Also, you can test their speed, and how quickly they respond now, will be the same as how quickly they will respond in the future. If I call my solicitor now, I will get through to him. If I email him, I expect a reply within 30 minutes, and the reason I expect this speed, is because of our client and solicitor history over many years.

Combining the expertise of these three professionals will result in a super smooth yet supercharged property acquisition.

CONVERSION TEAM

So now that you have the people in your team to acquire the property, you now need a conversion and refurbishment team on hand to strategically better the specification of your investment property.

When you start you will need one standard team of tradesmen that you can use. I have got to the stage where I have five refurbishment teams continuously working on projects, and I have had to hire a project manager to control the refurbishment process.

I mention this to show you that as time goes on, and you buy more and more property, you will have no choice but to hire a project manager as it will save you masses of time and energy.

Just as I have done above for you, I will share what you need to look for in order to find a good conversion or refurbishment team.

1. Can they show you current projects? This is an important criteria on this checklist. You do not want to work with any refurbishment team who cannot show you projects they have completed, or are in the process of completing. If they say no to this request, what does that tell you about the refurbishment team? Can you trust them to do the right job?

   What do they charge? You can get a feel for the market by shopping around. Compare the prices of what different teams charge for the job; as a minimum, obtain three estimates.

   There are two extremes to the spectrum of a refurbishment team. On one end a very high price, where you may be paying for the brand and larger organisation, and on the other end a very low price, where you will be paying for their inexperience and unprofessionalism, and are probably reliant on just one person to do the job.

   Ideally what works well is a local builder, who has all the tradesmen available, and charges a fair price to efficiently complete refurbishment, and this is what you should aim for when you begin.

   If you're like me and your portfolio grows and you decide to accelerate the acquisition process, you are able provide regular work for your refurbishment teams. We work so closely with our refurbishment teams that we receive a price discount of between 25% to 75% compared to what the market is charging. This is due to the working with our teams over the long term, and the trust they put in us to always have work available for them, and it's a win-win situation for all.

You will eventually begin to gain economies of scale when you are on your 10th or 11th property and you will need a regular team.

2. What is their timescale for the job? This is very important. This is because some teams charge per day, and some charge per contract. If the timescale for a certain job is two weeks, you must make sure that the team who is being paid daily has completed their job in two weeks, otherwise it will lead to costs spiralling out of control.

3. Similarly, you do not want to contract your refurbishment teams, and have them say that the job will take a month, when really it takes one to two weeks. So once again first shop around for price estimates, the timescales different teams are offering to get your work completed by, and choose one after you have completed your due diligence.

LETTING AGENTS

Using the services of a letting agent is an excellent way to tenant and manage your property. Now is the time for you to begin reaping the reward of residual passive income and have extra money 'in your pocket' every month.

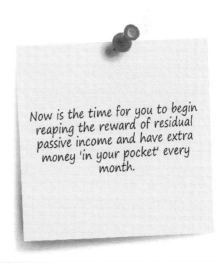

Now is the time for you to begin reaping the reward of residual passive income and have extra money 'in your pocket' every month.

I have seen many investors make a huge mistake here; they think they can manage the property themselves, collect rent on time, and carry on buying property.

Unfortunately it does not work like that. A good letting agent will manage this for you, and when you have developed a large enough portfolio, realistically, only then should you consider setting up your own letting agency.

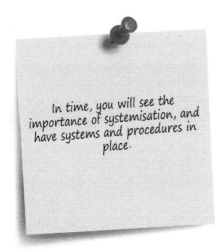

In time, you will see the importance of systemisation, and have systems and procedures in place.

This is because in time, you will see the importance of systemisation, and have systems and procedures in place so you are not involved.

Otherwise you are creating another job for yourself: dealing with tenants, collecting rent, managing repairs, and resolving late payment issues.

So in this part of chapter two, we have now discovered who you must have in your team to become a successful property investor. We have looked at the entire spectrum from acquisition to lettings, so you can now confidently use the ideas in this part of the chapter to go and find your winning team.

PROVEN SYSTEM

In order to become a successful property investor, you must have a proven system.

This system will allow you to leverage what you do, so that you can accelerate results and at the same time minimise mistakes. However, this proven system comes after a period of trial and improvement, and even today, I am consistently improving the systems I have so that it becomes even more efficient.

The aim is to achieve fast, long term and sustainable results each time it is implemented.

Now, the system I have created has been nurtured refined and grown over the last two and a half decades, using the knowledge gained from my seven-figure businesses and consistently acquiring and managing the whole property process.

I am continuously improving the system by learning from mentors who have multimillion and billion pounds of net worth, and who are learning from their mentors too.

This system is the 171 step ACT Formula. This system is used for our clients at Premier Portfolio Builder, where we manage the complete property process for them, all the way from sourcing and acquisition to the lettings and management. If you would like to know more about the services Premier Portfolio Builder offer, and you feel that there is a match, go to *www.PremierPortfolioBuilder.co.uk* and contact us through the website.

So this formula is broken down in to three parts: the acquisition, the conversion and refurbishment, and then the lettings. I will now share with you the information you need in each part to create a system.

You will find The Complete ACT Formula in the free workbook which you can download online from the following link: *www.PremierPortfolioBuilder.co.uk/workbook*

ACQUIRE

In the acquisition part of the system you need to include all the information, from sourcing the property to completion.

The first thing you must know is your exit strategy. Do you exit by selling the property and realising the profit, or is it by keeping the property over time and allowing the rent to pay all ongoing costs for the property?

You need to know where you want to invest and what channels you are going to use to find properties that match your criteria, for example estate agents.

Once you know where you are going to find the property, you need to know what type of property you are going to be buying. What I mean by this is the size, number of rooms, or number of floors, because you want to find a property where economically the numbers work so you are making a profit.

As soon as you know what property you are looking for, the area it is in, and the channel from which you will purchase the property, you now need to know how to finance the property, so that you can purchase it quickly, and there are many finance strategies out there.

Your winning team is also included in your system, as they will need to be available at the right times in order to make the acquisition process silky smooth.

CONVERT

As soon as you have collated together the acquisition part of the system, then it comes to the conversion and refurbishment part. For this, you will have your winning team ready to do the job. The first angle you need to look at when it comes to a refurbishment is what specification the refurbishment is going to be. A specification is the requirement to which the property needs to be refurbished or converted in order to be considered as a rentable property in that particular area. One of the aspects of the specification you must know is if it is a high end or budget specification, as this plays a very important part in renting your property. If you are in an area where they expect a low specification, and you give them a high specification, you have spent more than required and alternatively if you give someone a low specification and you are in a high specification area you will have challenges renting the property.

Second to that, regardless of the specification, there are certain parts of a refurbishment you want to avoid if possible, which will lead to unnecessary costs and you put these in your system. You do however want to include as many value addition strategies as possible. As soon as you know this, you then need to calculate the timescale the project will take, and you

Include as many value addition strategies as possible.

include this in there, as a certain type of refurbishment will take longer than others.

TENANTING

Once you have pieced together the acquisition and conversion and refurbishment part for the system, the final part is the lettings. This is where you will begin to receive your residual income from property.

The first thing you must know are the rental figures in your area, and know what is a realistic cash flow goal to achieve. This will vary from area to area, and from the type of property you buy. You can find these by visiting a letting agent.

You need to know your detailed tenant profile, and how to acquire them and manage them over a long period of time, and you will need a system if you are thinking of managing this part yourself. Ultimately, clarity over the type of tenant that fits your property and area will reduce voids. A letting agent can help you with this also.

Now you know what you must have in order to become a very successful property investor. In the next chapter we will go more into depth about the ACT Formula, so you can see and appreciate the depth to which a formula can go into.

KEY LEARNINGS

1. Never have only one person in each position of your winning team.

2. Your winning team will be developed over time.

3. The single let strategy will provide you a long term residual income and future capital growth.

4. Look carefully at the realistic figures when comparing strategies.

5. Know the costs at each stage of the property process, all the way through the property process.

6. Consider very carefully the capital growth and monthly income potential for the area you are investing in.

7. Communication is key in each part of the process.

8. If someone does a job better than you, let them do it. It will save you time, money and a lot of pain.

9. Build a system as you go along your journey.

10. Learn patience, as experience comes with time, and knowledge is a great starting point.

WORKBOOK

For your convenience, I have put all the exercises into an easy-to-download and easy-to-print PDF workbook because it's better than writing in this book.

You can download your workbook here:
www.PremierPortfolioBuilder.co.uk/workbook

CHAPTER 3

ACQUIRING PROPERTY

THE ACT FORMULA

Now we are going to go into more depth about getting a better understanding of how to build a successful property portfolio. The first part of the formula is the acquisition part, and there are many different features you must look at about a property before you consider acquiring it.

Property is a great asset class, and the single let strategy is a great strategy, but you also need a great amount of knowledge to make it a success.

Property is a great asset class, and the single let strategy is a great strategy, but you also need a huge amount of knowledge to make it a success. So in this part we will look at the acquisition part of the formula.

FINDING THE RIGHT LOCATION

The first objective you need to complete before you purchase your property is finding the right location to invest in. It takes a lot of time and research in order to find the correct areas, and I have seen many investors lose a lot of money because they invested in the wrong areas.

The reason location is key is because you are looking for an area that will be suitable for you for the long term, and an area that supports your goals on boosting your income and pension. Before I reveal how to find the right location, I would just like to add that there are people out there who produce wonderful marketing material on why investing in a certain area provides a fantastic result.

So please make sure you do your due diligence on the area very thoroughly before investing there. So let's look at a few of the main factors you must research in order to find the right location.

HIGH GROWTH POTENTIAL

The first way to find the right location is through finding out if that area has a high potential to grow. You want to make sure that the area you invest in is not in a declining, flat or minimal growth market because this is not long term thinking.

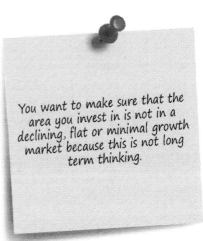

You want to make sure that the area you invest in is not in a declining, flat or minimal growth market because this is not long term thinking.

As time goes on, you want the value of your property to increase. There are a few ways in which you can check the potential growth of an area.

One way is to look at the amount of funding that is being deployed in the area. There are different types of funding, for example how much funding is going into the regeneration project that is happening in the area. If there is a large regeneration project occurring, for example where I invest for myself and where my company invests for our clients, we are in an area which is part of the largest regeneration project in Europe, so this means that over time property prices will potentially increase at an accelerated rate compared to other areas in the country.

Another type of funding would be the government spending in the area to improve the skills of the work force. This is important, because from an economic perspective, if the labour work force is getting more and more educated, this means that they are more likely to get a job, which results in unemployment decreasing.

Therefore if unemployment decreases, this means more individuals in that micro economy will have more disposable income, which will result in them spending more, so consumption will also increase in that micro economy.

This will cause an increase in value for that micro economy.

Aside from funding, another way to know if the area you are about to be investing in has the potential to be a high growth area is through the infrastructure in place there.

There are different types of infrastructure that you can have. One of the major types of infrastructure is transport links. In the area you invest you want there to be established transport links in place, and you need those to be in place now.

If it is just an idea or projection, there is no guarantee that it will occur in the future.

You certainly wouldn't want to build your financial viability around such a prediction.

More importantly, you need to make sure the transport links are linked to London, because that is where the major growth is happening.

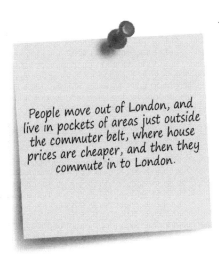

People move out of London, and live in pockets of areas just outside the commuter belt, where house prices are cheaper, and then they commute in to London.

As property prices in London are on average higher than the UK average, this means people move out of London, and live in pockets of areas just outside the commuter belt, where house prices are cheaper, and then they commute in to London. For example, where I invest, you can get to London by train in just 30 minutes.

Ideally you want the train into London to take less than 45 minutes, because that would probably be the typical amount of time someone would want to spend commuting into London.

To strengthen that point further, you must also check the cost of commuting into London, as some areas have transport links in place where it may seem as if you can get in to London in a reasonable time. However the cost of the commute is very high. This is a false economy and an average person would see that the cost of commute does not justify the commuting journey time.

RENTAL DEMAND

So now you know how to find an area where there is high potential growth, you need to make sure that there is going to be demand for your property in the rental market.

The rental demand aspect of building a successful property portfolio is very important, as the cash flow from your property will act as your income and pension.

So you want to make sure that you can maximise on the amount of income you achieve through having your property rented at all times. For you to be in an area where the rental demand is good, you want there to be a shortage of houses, because then there will be an excess of tenants.

This means there is demand for your property, and over time, as tenant competition increases, your rental income will also potentially increase. In order to know whether there truly is a demand in the rental market in your area, you need to complete the following actions.

The first action you need to take is to go and visit a minimum of three letting agents and see the properties that they have available to rent. Go in to the office and ask them what the demand is like, they will generally give you a truthful answer.

You can also ask them for certain figures such as number of viewings per property, the time taken from listing a rental property to it being rented, and the length of the void period if the tenant leaves.

This way you will begin to get a clearer idea as to whether

the area you are investing in will provide you a long term low risk sustainable income.

The second way to discover if there is a rental demand in the area you are about to invest is by viewing some rental properties on websites online and tracking how many days it takes for the property to go from to let to rented.

Also, by comparing rental properties online, you can begin to get a feel for the amount of rent that is achievable in your area, so you can then work out the calculations for what will work and what will not.

The third way to see if there is rental demand is to go to your local council and ask them for a waiting list of people who are waiting for housing. The longer the list, the better this is for you.

This is because, if there are masses of people waiting for housing, you can select the best tenants to go in to your property and they will pay you the correct rent because there are not enough properties available for rent in that area.

WHERE TO INVEST IN THE UK

We have now discussed the rental demand and the potential for high growth areas, so where actually in the UK is the best area to start? From the criteria I have written above, there are a handful of locations across the UK. To help you to achieve complete clarity on which area to invest in, you need to look at the UK as a whole and then begin to focus on certain areas.

Typically the area you invest comes down to the "north-south divide" in the UK, which we will now consider further and look at the major differences between the north and south. Let's look at the north first.

Typically the north brings higher yields, and cash flow. This is because the average property prices there are much lower, therefore the yield looks better.

However, the north has a slower economic growth compared to the south, and especially compared to the south east.

The reason for the slower growth is due to the fact that government expenditure on key areas such as infrastructure is much lower in the north compared to the south, and the average income is a lot lower in the north.

This means that people would not want to relocate there because, firstly, the infrastructure in place may be at a lower standard, and in some parts key types of infrastructure may not be in place, and secondly, because of the fact that the income is lower.

That being said, there are some pockets in the north that may have the potential to be good investment areas, however then the purchase price would be too high, so the yield would be too low.

Now we have evaluated the north, let's evaluate the south. The south and especially the south east is nearer to London. Due to London being the one of the major financial centres of the world, which has excellent infrastructure and great heritage in place, London is the centre of attraction for many. London is the capital city and the financial hub of the UK, and this attracts a lot of interest from foreign nationals, who invest their capital into London.

London has outstanding educational establishments, with centuries of history. So the nearer to London you are, the higher the capital appreciation is. The further you go out of London, the lower the capital appreciation is.

This is due to the ripple effect. The ripple effect in property works similar to the ripple effect that happens when you throw a pebble in to the water, the ripples begin around the centre of the pebble, but these ripples spread much further out.

The ripple effect in property works similar to the ripple effect that happens when you throw a pebble in to the water, the ripples begin around the centre of the pebble, but these ripples spread much further out.

The same is true for property. London is the city that everyone wants to buy in and the highest prices are in London, but if you use the ripple analogy as you go out 10 or 20 miles from London, the prices tend to get lower, yet are still guided by London growth. Therefore if we buy in the centre of the 'ripples', i.e. London, the prices are really too high and the yields are too low.

However, on the outskirts of the ripple, the prices are lower and yields are higher. This falls in to the Greater London urban area region or the edge of London as I like to call it. When there is growth appreciation in London, the ripple effect makes sure this happens for the outer ripples or outer regions as well.

So if you look at areas 20 to 30 miles outside London,

you are able to identify locations that work really well for building your property portfolio, giving excellent benefits with the advantage of capital appreciation. By looking at the ripple effect, you have simply found the balance between capital appreciation and yield.

This is why I invest in the south east of England. From evaluating the areas above, I believe that we can come to the conclusion that the south of England and especially the south east of England are definitely the safest, tried and tested areas to be investing in.

However, now that you know the region of the country that is most beneficial for you to secure your long term financial future, you now need to focus further in to the towns within those regions. Once you discovered the correct towns, then you need to focus on the micro areas within those towns.

Each town has streets which are underperforming for investments purposes and other streets which are exceptionally good for investment.

In fact, you will discover you are now focusing your time and energy on a number of specific streets. Each town has streets which are underperforming for investments purposes, and other streets which are exceptionally good for investment. You want to make sure you find the best possible streets to invest in that are aligned with your long term plans.

ANALYSE PROFITABILITY

Profitability is very important in any business. This is why, when it comes to property, you want to make sure you can calculate the important facts and figures.

Property is statistically proven to be the most expensive asset class we invest in in our lifetime, and yet some people take huge risks in property without the correct knowledge, experience and teams.

> Property is statistically proven to be the most expensive asset class we invest in, in our life time, and yet some people take huge risks in property without the correct knowledge, experience and teams.

If you are reading this book and have made unfortunate decisions in property in the past you will be able to relate to this. If you are this person, I would like to acknowledge your courage for reading this book, and if you are like me, it's all about persistence until you find a path that's right for you.

The reality of the property world is that, yes, there is a lot of money to be made, if you know the strategies, and have the contacts, experience and knowledge.

However, there is also a lot of money to be lost if you take an amateur approach, which is how some property investors' horror stories come about. Some people are naive in their approach to property investing, and I would not recommend that at all.

You must make sure your numbers are safe, secure and

completely solid, or you are just gambling. Therefore in order to be a smart and successful investor, there are three key parts of profitability which you must consider in order to ensure that your investment is safe, robust and risk averse, and at the same time sustainable for the long term.

You must make sure your numbers are safe, secure and completely solid, or you are just gambling.

RENTAL YIELD

The first type of calculation you need to look at is the rental yield, which is an income calculation.

The rental yield is one that takes into account the purchase price, your annual rent that you will achieve for the year, all costs such as mortgage fees, solicitors' fees, and any other fees. (Refurbishment costs are not included in this calculation as these are capital calculations which I will show you later on.)

The rental yield is split into two calculations; you have the gross rental yield and the net rental yield. The gross rental yield is the yield inclusive of costs, and the net rental yield is the gross rental yield minus the costs.

The way to calculate yield is by multiplying your rent value per calendar month by 12 and then dividing that by the purchase price of the property.

Once you have this value, you multiply it by 100 to calculate a percentage. This will give you a gross yield value. The net yield value is calculated by first working out your rent value per calendar month, so that would be your rent minus expenses such as mortgages, maintenance and insurance.

The net value you calculate for the month you then multiply by 12 – this gives you an annual amount, which is then divided by the purchase price of the property.

RETURN ON INVESTMENT

The second type of calculation is the return on investment, which is a capital calculation. This is more of an accurate calculation as it looks at the amount of money you have put into a property to make it work.

This is because professional property investors leverage and use a mortgage in order to buy an asset which is worth multiple times the deposit that they put in to purchase the property.

Professional property investors leverage and use a mortgage in order to buy an asset which is worth multiple times the deposit that they put in to purchase the property.

For example, if you have a property valued at £125,000 the bank will be able to give you a mortgage on the property, as property is seen as a safe investment by the banks. Normally, a bank will lend you 75% of the property value, and in this case the total amount they are likely to lend you is £93,750. This means that you will only need to put in a deposit of £31,250 to purchase the property, which is 25% of the value of the property. This results in you being able to purchase an asset which is worth four times more than what you have put in, as you have only put in £31,250 to purchase a property worth £125,000.

Then you add on other costs, such as refurbishment costs, legal fees, mortgage fees and other fees to your deposit. After you have done that, you work out the annual gross rental amount and annual net rental amount, which I shared with you in the rental calculation above.

Then you divide these annual figures by the total amount of capital you have put in to make the property work for you.

CAPITAL EXPENDITURE

The next type of calculation is to do with the amount of capital you actually spend on a property. This calculation will show whether the total costs for acquiring the property reflect whether the property is a good investment decision.

The capital expenditure includes any refurbishment costs, stamp duty fees, professional service fees such as solicitors' fees, mortgage arrangement fees, project management fees, and any other costs.

You will find all these calculations in the free workbook which you can download online from the following link: www.PremierPortfolioBuilder.co.uk/workbook

ACQUIRE THE PROPERTY

Now you have discovered how to find the correct area to buy in and how to make sure that the calculations for an investment property work for you, you now need to understand which strategy you can implement to actually acquire the property.

For someone who is starting in property, there are three main acquisition channels, and each one has its advantages and disadvantages. I have personally used these strategies many times for myself and the people I have worked with, and here are the advantages and disadvantages of each.

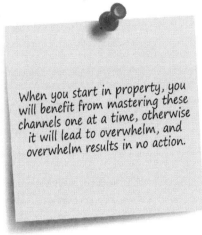

When you start in property, you will benefit from mastering these channels one at a time, otherwise it will lead to overwhelm, and overwhelm results in no action.

When you start in property, you will benefit from mastering these channels one at a time, otherwise it will lead to overwhelm, and overwhelm results in no action. You will benefit from being clear on the acquisition channel you want to pursue.

Once you have acquired around 15 to 20 properties, you will learn, develop and create a structure that works for you for that particular acquisition channel. Once you have created a successful and sustainable structure, you can move on to the next relevant acquisition strategy.

ACQUISITION VIA ESTATE AGENTS

The first acquisition channel is to acquire property through an estate agent. When I mention the words "estate agents" to some investors who are just about to begin their journey, their heart begins to race, their face goes pale, and they courageously put on a nervous smile.

The reason this happens is because of the fear of dealing with estate agents. The first thing about estate agents is that they are people, just like you and me – they are just doing their job.

My team and I work with all the key estate agencies in our investment area, on a regular basis. This means we must be in contact with at least 20-25 estate agents each month.

So let us evaluate the advantages and disadvantages of acquiring property through estate agents, and I will share with you a few tactics to find a good estate agent so that you can acquire property from them continuously just like me.

The first advantage of acquiring property through the estate agent is they are practically a consultant working for you for free, and therefore you are able to receive an instant insight in to the market. Through talking to agents, you get the feel of where prices are moving to, how much a property should be costing you and in general how the area is growing as a whole.

> An advantage of acquiring property through the estate agent is they are practically a consultant working for you for free.

The second advantage of estate agents is that after you find your area, and you know how to make the calculations work, you can then teach them what kind of properties you are looking for and acquire the correct investment properties.

If you are reliable and trustworthy, they will listen to you, and they will be happy to work with you.

If you were the agent, and I was the buyer, you know that you can rely on me to make the purchase as I am a serious person when it comes to delivering what I promise, and therefore that means that ultimately you can trust me and that is what the estate agent is ultimately looking for.

For example if you were the agent, and I was the buyer, you know that you can rely on me to make the purchase as I am a serious person when it comes to delivering what I promise, and therefore that means that ultimately you can trust me and that is what the estate agent is looking for.

These are the two main advantages of buying property through an estate agent, and they are definitely very big advantages. However, as well as advantages there are disadvantages.

One disadvantage is that it takes a lot of time effort and resources to be able to build rapport with your agents. You may need to buy three four, five, or even ten properties from them before they even begin to listen to you.

This is because each estate agent has an exclusive list of investors they call first when the correct property comes up, but this list is not something that is publicised. If you are like me and my team, your name will be at the top of that exclusive list, as you are someone who the estate agent will trust. The only way to get on to that list is through purchasing property quickly, reliably, and continuously.

The second disadvantage is that you do not want to be dealing with any agent in the office, and I see many investors fall down here because the agent that they go and speak to first is the one that will take on their file.

So you need to find the estate agent in that agency that is going to help you achieve your long term plans by acquiring the correct investment properties, and this will allow you to boost your pension and income.

Over time, your relationship within the agency will develop from the agent you are dealing with to the whole office, and then from the whole office to the whole area, and then eventually from the whole area to the district. As soon as the district is aware of you, you will then be the go to person for them

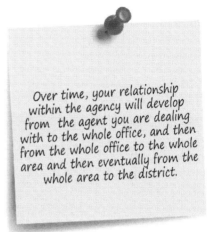

Over time, your relationship within the agency will develop from the agent you are dealing with to the whole office, and then from the whole office to the whole area and then eventually from the whole area to the district.

every time there is the correct investment property.

The third disadvantage of an agent is you have to remember they are not your friend. They are sales people to begin with, and they may not share everything with you.

They may hide certain aspects of a property, or the issues that certain streets present, or involve you in a bidding war, which is why you must do your own due diligence on the property and on the area. The estate agent is there to earn a living, and the more properties they sell, the more commissions they will make – it is a numbers game for them.

Only when you have been working with them for a period

of time will you earn their respect and when you reach that pivotal point they will consider you as a friend or colleague.

The final disadvantage I would like to share with you about buying through an estate agent is that estate agencies tend to have a high staff turnover. Therefore you could build a relationship with a particular agent, but generally an agent will stay in an office for between a year to 18 months, and that means you have to start the whole process again.

ACQUISITION DIRECTLY FROM THE VENDOR

The second type of property acquisition channel is to purchase the property directly from the vendor. This type of strategy may be more time and effort intensive; however it will produce excellent results for you.

The main advantage of buying direct from the vendor is it will allow you to secure properties which are not on the market, i.e. off market properties. Other investors may not have seen these properties advertised, therefore the competition from other property investors is heavily reduced. This means that you will not have to participate in a bidding war, where the price just keeps increasing higher and higher and the real figures needed for a correct investment begin to diminish and work less and less.

The reason for the property being off market is because the vendor may not like estate agents or other property selling professionals, as they may find them intimidating to deal with. However, they are happy to speak to someone like you to buy their property. The second advantage is that it saves you time because there isn't a middle man.

By going direct to the vendor, you are immediately in contact with the person who is selling their house; therefore it is beneficial to you as you will save time in the process between offering a purchase price, and the price being accepted as you do not have to communicate through a third party such as an estate agent.

The third advantage is as they know there is no middle man the costs are going to be lower for them to sell their property. This is because they will not have to pay the estate agent any commission, and therefore you will have the opportunity to negotiate a better price.

The fourth advantage is you will build rapport with the vendor as they are dealing directly with you and not just a cold, faceless buyer who they do not know. In this scenario, they will get to know, like and trust you, which means that they will choose you to buy their property. This means that other buyers will not be able to outbid you during the transaction between you and the seller.

The fifth advantage is more for self-gratification rather than profit purposes. When you go and see that vendor, and you find out why they are selling their home, you will realise that you are helping them move on.

Generally, these types of home owners will be going through some rather distressing situations in their life. This means that by you being able to buy their property, you are allowing them to move on with their life, and helping them escape from repossession, debt, or even helping them relocate to another area or country because of a job or family reasons.

Now let's consider the disadvantages of this strategy.

First of all, going directly to the vendor can be quite distressing for you. If you are listening to the vendor's problems it may affect you psychologically and you may not find this a pleasurable experience.

Secondly, to achieve the best results you will need a team. When you buy direct to vendor, there are different strategies, such as leaflets, postcards, and other creative marketing techniques. This means that you will need to build a marketing team.

If you choose to do this yourself it will be very time intensive, and you will lose a lot of your precious time or you will need to be doing this as a full time or 'very' part time career.

Equally, if you paid someone to do it for you, it may be quite expensive, so there is a trade-off for you to make a decision, and it really comes down to working out what your time is really worth as a monetary value.

The last disadvantage I will mention here is if you are a more systematic, operational and more analytically inclined, the skills you have are a real asset to you, however for this channel if you don't like dealing with people and their problems, this channel will be a disadvantage.

ACQUIRING VIA AUCTION

Now you know the advantages and disadvantages of buying through an estate agent and buying directly from the vendor, we are going to look at the acquisition channel that involves buying via auction.

There are many auction houses up and down the country, and if you haven't been to one, it is definitely a good experience to go and visit to see what the atmosphere and the bidding is like.

Like the two acquisition channels already mentioned, this channel also has its advantages and disadvantages.

One advantage is that going to auction allows you to pick up great opportunities. What I mean by this is, personally, I don't go to auction houses to buy a property; I go to an auction house looking for a piece of land with planning permission to put eight to ten houses on there, or a piece of land that has the potential to be built upon to produce a block of flats, so going to auction is great for these types of opportunities.

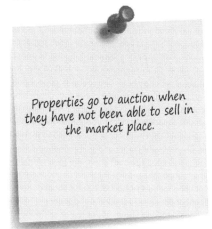

Properties go to auction when they have not been able to sell in the market place.

However the disadvantages of obtaining a property via auction is that it can be extremely costly. The first is actually to do with the properties. Generally I have found that properties go to auction when they have not been able to sell in the market place.

This may be due to the fact there are some structural issues, or problems in the area. The second disadvantage of an auction is the excited mood it gets you in. At auctions I have seen too many investors pay way over the asking price for the property, because they are involved in a live bidding war.

In this atmosphere, no person wants to lose, and the ego is let loose because people around them are watching. What I would recommend is if you do go to auction, and the prices are way above what you would pay, just simply walk out of the room. It is better to leave than to lose thousands of pounds through buying a property in an area and at a cost where the figures do not stack up.

The third disadvantage would relate to the market you are in. Right now, the price of property in the south east and London is rising. Therefore, when you go to an auction in a rising market, there will be flocks and flocks of amateur investors ready to get on the property ladder, which means the competition is fierce at an auction. However, in a market where the media is not talking about the massive buzz in the property market, there will be less completion, therefore you are better off by visiting then. I would buy properties at auction in the correct part of the property cycle, which may mean this channel will have to wait for three to five years.

The last disadvantage of an auction is that many people do not view the property before they purchase it. They just turn up to the auction, view a couple of pictures and then they are ready to go. For an auction purchase please make sure that you go and view the property, ideally with your builder so that they can see what kind of works the property will need for in order for it to be made into a fantastic investment property.

So now we have discussed the advantages and disadvantages of the three acquisition channels, it is now up to you to decide which one is best for you. Like I said earlier, if you are beginning, an estate agent may be for you. If you are experienced, and have maybe 50 to 60 plus properties you may look to go to auction to purchase that piece of land to develop on. Whichever the acquisition channel is, choose one, and become an expert in that. Then when you have become an expert in one, move on to the next acquisition channel.

KEY LEARNINGS

1. Do your due diligence on an area before you buy.

2. Once you find your area, begin to focus on the best streets.

3. Find an area with high growth potential.

4. Find an area with good infrastructure.

5. Find an area close to London to invest in.

6. Make sure there is enough rental demand for your area.

7. Always make sure the capital expenditure does not adversely affect your calculations.

8. Always calculate the return on investment as well as yield.

9. Remember estate agents like to work with preferred buyers who perform.

10. Auction properties may be incompletely described – always go and visit the auction property.

11. Direct to vendor strategy has a trade-off between cost and time.

12. Become an expert in one acquisition channel and then move on to another following acquisition channel.

WORKBOOK

For your convenience, I have put all the exercises into an easy-to-download and easy-to-print PDF workbook because it's better than writing in this book.

You can download your workbook here:
www.PremierPortfolioBuilder.co.uk/workbook

CHAPTER 4

CONVERTING OR REFURBISHING A PROPERTY

The next part of the ACT Formula is the conversion and refurbishment section. Any conversion or refurbishment should be planned and outlined at the onset when you have agreed to acquire the property. This section becomes the primary focus after you have acquired the property and the property is now legally yours.

The conversion refurbishment section of the ACT Formula is very important, as if this is not carried out correctly, there could be some serious long term implications such as:

1. Longer than expected void periods as it may be difficult to find tenants.

2. Increased maintenance over time if any current maintenance issues aren't dealt with.

3. Local authority taking action if the property does not conform to current health and safety rules and regulations.

It is important you maximise on opportunities that allow you to add value to the property, increasing its market value and therefore increasing the equity in your property.

I will now share some strategies to increase the value of the property, and some tips and ideas to make sure any conversions and refurbishments are carried out correctly.

PROPERTY CONVERSION

When I mention conversion, I am talking about making non-structural changes and/or floor plan changes to the layout of the property.

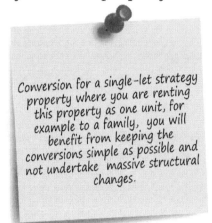

Conversion for a single-let strategy property where you are renting this property as one unit, for example to a family, you will benefit from keeping the conversions simple as possible and not undertake massive structural changes.

In a conversion for a single-let strategy property where you are renting this property as one unit, for example to a family, you will benefit from keeping the conversions as simple as possible and not undertaking massive structural changes as it is not worth your time, effort and resources.

So, here are three value-addition strategies that you can use in order to add value to your property, and at the same time allow your property to achieve a higher rental income, and lower void periods.

Before you begin the conversion, you want to make sure that the conversion will make financial sense once completed.

A fantastic way to measure this is by finding out how much the monthly rental will increase and by dividing the cost of works by this rental figure. This way you can work out how long it will take for you to recoup the cost of the conversion.

This will clearly help you decide whether it makes sense to do the conversion. You will find this calculation in the free online workbook you can download. You will also find examples of floor plans for the following conversions in the free workbook:

RELOCATE BATHROOM

The first type of conversion in your property can be to relocate the bathroom to another area of the property. For example a two bedroom house with an upstairs bathroom can be converted in to a three bedroom house if space can be found on the ground floor and the bathroom is moved downstairs.

A two bedroom house with an upstairs bathroom, can be converted in to a three bedroom house if space can be found on the ground floor.

You have increased the value of the property by doing this and increased the rent you will receive. It is important that you check that the tenant profile fits with having a downstairs bathroom and that it is acceptable before you carry out the bathroom relocation conversion, and in most areas this is fine.

CREATING ADDITIONAL ROOMS

Some properties have large rooms and large cupboard spaces that can be reconfigured. Where there are non-load-bearing walls, these can be partitioned to create extra rooms. This could be as simple as dividing a large bedroom into two, creating an extra bedroom.

Values are aligned with number of rooms rather than the overall floor area, which is a great advantage to you as a property investor.

This increases the value of the property because, unlike other countries, values are aligned with number of rooms rather than the overall floor area, which is a great advantage to you as a property investor.

Yet, do be aware of minimum room sizes and requirements for window sizes, all of which you can check online with your local council.

LOFT CONVERSION

This is another fantastic way to add value to a property, by using the loft space which usually is a redundant space. Please be aware that you will need to check with your local council for permitted development of a loft; you may need planning approval and it is best to work out your return on investment by measuring rent and value increase to the property.

There are a number of other conversions that are more cash intensive, and require involvement from building control and local council planning departments.

My recommendation to you is to be aware of the potential of what is achievable with your property, so you can carry out these conversions at a later date. You only carry out the conversion process if the return on your investment makes calculated sense. A way to check this is to work out the total profit that extra conversion makes you over three years. If the cost of the conversion is equal to or less than the profit gained from the conversion, then you should go ahead with it.

Some conversions to consider if you are an experienced investor:

- Garage conversion

- Back extension

- Two storey extension

- Removing chimney breasts and structural walls

- Converting a house into a number of flats

- Developing new buildings on land belonging to the current property

PROPERTY REFURBISHMENT PROCESS

The aim is to provide good quality accommodation that meets your tenant profile, and it is important you keep this in focus that it is an investment property and not your own personal residence. In our property business we make sure for every £1 spent we add £3 in value to the property and avoid any structural changes.

For example, painting a wall is a refurbishment, whereas moving a staircase is a structural change, and therefore a conversion in my opinion.

A refurbishment is a great way to add value to a property and create demand for your property. However unnecessary works to the property can mean increased costs which will eat into your profits.

It is critical that this section is completed correctly, and there is a discipline on the capital expenditure and what works are carried out. It is very important you have the correct refurbishment team to do the job correctly.

In our business we have five full time refurbishment teams in-house, but it wasn't always like that, and you have to start somewhere. Here are some tips on finding a great refurbishment team.

You can get recommendations from other investors, estate agents and letting agents. I cannot emphasise enough how much a recommendation can benefit you, because recommendations mean that the work has been completed to a satisfactory standard.

Always obtain estimates from at least three builders; this way you will be able to gauge the correct costs by comparing Another benefit of this is that you will gain experience from the builder on what needs to be done to a property. Each time you have a conversation with a different builder you learn something new, and this is a way to build up your own experience.

When looking for refurbishment teams be aware that you should be looking for someone who is capable of doing the job, and have a budget set aside for this.

You may find smaller local builders will be more cost effective than larger firms, as their overheads are lower, and can make the decision on pricing your refurbishment and not have to be rigid in their pricing or have to go to their line manager to agree a price.

Now you know what needs to be looked at in order to refurbish a property, you may be thinking "How can I refurbish a property if I have a very tight budget?" Here are a few super-secret strategies my team and I implement when it comes to refurbishing a property on a strict budget, and it's important to focus on the specific areas within a property.

There are three key areas in the property that will need the most attention:

THE KITCHEN

Now, an amateur investor will walk into the property and completely rip out the kitchen without any hesitation, and fit in a new one for thousands of pounds. Here's what my team and I do differently.

Once you have tenanted your property, you want a hassle-free long term income, and low maintenance in the kitchen really helps.

There are six aspects of the kitchen we check, and the first one we check is the floor. It is important your investment property is low maintenance, and that ongoing maintenance is easy to do.

For this reason I recommend a good quality vinyl flooring and not tiling. The advantage of this is when tenants move out or if any repairs are required to the floor, vinyl can simply be lifted up, or removed and replaced, and maintenance becomes easier for you. The second reason is because vinyl is easy to clean; if something is spilt, or a mark is left on vinyl flooring it can be cleaned relatively easily. The final reason is because of its longevity.

Tiling will cost you more money further down the line during the management and lettings process if tiles break or need to be replaced, or if there is any maintenance to the floor.

However, whether there is vinyl or tiling on the floor, before you decide to replace it, check whether you can just clean the floor. If you can clean the flooring, and can restore it back to a good standard, you can save money.

A property investor I was mentoring recently believed this would only save her a small amount of money, and the key learning for her was that by calculating all the small savings throughout her property the total sum saved was quite substantial and was actually five months of her net income from the property.

After you have inspected the floor, the second part of the kitchen to check is the kitchen units. Before you rip out all of the units, are you able to clean and polish the units to restore them to a good standard? If so, you will save yourself a lot of costs.

Alternatively, if you have to replace the units, do you need to replace all of them? Or is it just one cabinet door? Or a drawer handle? These are all parts to check before you carry out the refurbishment. When you have checked the units, the third part of the kitchen you then check is the work top.

If the work top is damaged, please do not try to cover this up. In this case, replace the work top completely. Simply changing the work top and cupboard doors can make the kitchen look new at a fraction of the cost.

The fourth part of the kitchen you check is the tap and basin. For this, you may just need to clean it to restore it to a good condition.

Alternatively, if you do have to replace this, you may just need to replace the tap. It really is about saving wherever possible, no matter how small the saving, because this all compounds over the whole refurbishment and how much you can save will really surprise you.

The key question to ask continuously: "Is it actually necessary to change this?"

Many tenants find the kitchen to be the focal point of their home, and it is important you get the look and feel right for your prospective tenant, always keeping your tenant profile in mind, knowing their needs.

Fifth, the tiling on the walls gives the kitchen a whole new, more expensive look. Your tenant will appreciate it a lot more, and it doesn't need to be expensive. The tiles need to be set in a way where there are ideally two colours, as it will make the kitchen look larger and at the same time fresh, clean and modern. A white tile is very cost effective, and an inexpensive border coordinated with the colour of the kitchen units adds character to the kitchen.

The sixth aspect is health and safety issues: hard wired smoke alarms and heat detectors, fire safety doors, and fire extinguisher and blanket are some of the standard items my team will put in every property. This is more of a minimum requirement and it is important that you safeguard people living in your property.

You will find before and after pictures of the refurbishments and conversions we carry out in the free workbook which you can download online from the following link: www.PremierPortfolioBuilder.co.uk/workbook

BREATHING LIFE INTO A TIRED BATHROOM

The next area in your property you need to check is the bathroom.

Generally, in a single let family home there is only one bathroom, which is either next to the kitchen or on the first floor. When it comes to the bathroom, you do not need to spend huge amounts to refurbish it, there just needs to be a simple, bright refurbishment that makes the bathroom look new, and adds value to your property.

For example by deep cleaning the bathroom, and cleaning the grout between wall tiles to restore it to a good condition, replacing any old silicone along the joints between the bathroom suite and the walls, and decorating the bathroom, this will save you both time and money. However, if you cannot, here is what you need to replace.

The first will be the flooring, and again it should be vinyl flooring as in the kitchen. If you have a carpet in a bathroom, make sure it is replaced, as this will cause you long term problems.

Secondly, in the bathroom the walls are very important. With the walls, you need to make sure that they are covered in a waterproof material. Tiling the walls in the bath area to ceiling height will remove problems with condensation to the walls.

Furthermore, to save you costs and time even further, you only need to tile half the bathroom where the water is likely to splash. Check the bathroom suite, including the toilet pan, bath and basin. In many cases, the toilet pan may not need replacing. You may just need to purchase a toilet seat, which will give the bathroom the same effect of a new toilet pan.

If you replace the bath, make sure it's a steel bath for low future maintenance. It will be much more robust than the acrylic baths, which crack over time.

You want a property to be occupied by tenants that live there for many years.

In order to do this, you must provide them with a refurbished property which has been completed to a long term standard. As the bathroom is a wet area you will find that ordinary paint will peel off the wall. Make sure when painting the bathroom that you use specialist bathroom paint and not the paint in the other rooms in the property.

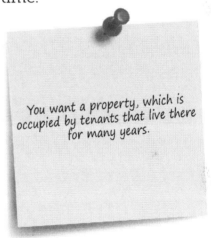

You want a property, which is occupied by tenants that live there for many years.

For electrical safety, the correct light fittings have to be used in the bathroom, and it is important you have a good quality extractor fan in the bathroom to help relieve condensation building up. Always seek advice from a credible electrician when making any electrical changes in your property.

STAGING THE PROPERTY AND DECORATING ON A BUDGET

It is important to see your property through prospective tenants' eyes.

Although it may seem strange, walk up to the property from the outside, then work your way through the property and then out the back of the property. When you walk up to the property, is the front garden clean? Are there hedges that need to be cut, and are there weeds that need to be ripped out?

Secondly, if there is a front garden gate, you may just need to paint it rather than replace it, and if the hinges are rusty, spraying with rust remover in the right areas will restore the gate back to its original standard.

Now as you open the gate and approach the door, does the door need replacing, or can you simply add cosmetic touch ups to breathe life back into the tired door? For example, many old houses have door number stickers on their front door. If you simply purchase chrome metal numbers, and screw these into the door, it will give the front of the property a brand new look. This means you have saved time and money rather than replacing the door completely.

Simply changing the door furniture can make the front of the door look attractive, and the front door is really a focal point for your property.

Also, when you check the windows on the front side of

the property, they may just need cleaning, which will save you a lot of money compared to replacing them with new windows.

So now you have observed the outside, let's open the door and explore the inside. When you step into the property, what is the first thing that you do? You take a deep breath in.

Make sure the property smells nice by leaving air fresheners around the property.

If there is a laminate or carpet flooring, can this be cleaned, or does it need to be replaced? If you are looking to replace the flooring, I would recommend carpet, as first of all it is less expensive than laminate flooring, and secondly like the vinyl flooring it is easy maintenance for the long term.

Thirdly, check the walls and ceilings. If the walls have wallpaper which is in a good standard, you may be able to paint over it, or if the wallpaper is tired, then removing it and re-plastering as necessary and painting the walls is a good option.

Painting completely transforms the feel in rooms.

Also, make sure you paint the ceiling. Painting completely transforms the feel in rooms, and each room becomes brighter. I recommend two coats of vinyl silk on the ceilings in white and two coats of magnolia coloured vinyl silk on the walls. I prefer vinyl silk as it is easy to clean and can simply be wiped over, and magnolia on walls creates a neutral space, and white on ceilings creates a feeling of more space. Any wood work, such as doors and skirting boards, should be painted in white non-drip gloss, which is quicker to apply.

Once you have checked the walls, next you need to check the fittings, for example, door handles and sockets, and light switches. By replacing these, your refurbishment looks great, and these are inexpensive items. In a single let family unit investment property, you will just need simple white coloured plastic sockets. Also, I would recommend replacing any broken door handles with chrome.

However, if all the door handles in the property are gold, and all but one is working, please only replace the one that is needed, because you have to spend less. This is the point when people tend to lose the discipline and spend more than they need to.

The last super-secret strategy is all to do with light bulbs. Before your tenant comes to view your property, replace all the light bulbs with 100 watt light bulbs. This is an amazing strategy, and it will make your refurbishment look even better, and also give the perception of more space and openness. You can simply replace these light bulbs with energy efficiency light bulbs for the tenants, which will keep the energy costs of your property lower, and I usually gift a complete set of light bulbs to the tenants as it's simply a nice touch for tenants who are moving in.

What I have learnt over the last two and a half decades of property investing is that the small amounts stack up, and a couple of pounds here and there will lead to thousands of pounds of overspending, so always watch the pennies and the pounds will look after themselves.

HOW TO AVOID MISTAKES

Now you know some of the value addition strategies that I use in both the conversion and refurbishment processes of the ACT Formula, I am now going to show you how to avoid the mistakes people make during these processes. If you want to make this part of the process a success, you must know some of the mistakes you need to stay away from. Many investors believe that because they have now acquired the property they now have an asset and they can relax.

This is not true. Your property is a liability until it has been tenanted. Once it has been tenanted, only then will your property truly be an asset, because you will be receiving ongoing income from the property. Therefore the refurbishment and conversion section of the formula lies between the acquisition and the tenanting, and is very important.

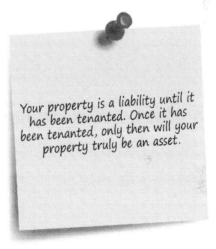

Your property is a liability until it has been tenanted. Once it has been tenanted, only then will your property truly be an asset.

SELECT A GREAT TEAM

This first way you can avoid mistakes is by selecting a great team. We discussed how to find a good refurbishment team in chapter two. There are many positives to selecting a great refurbishment and conversion team.

The first is that they know what they have to do as they are experts in their field. You are able to show them the property. Show them a specification to what standard you want it to, and they should be able to do the job to that exact standard, if not better.

By selecting a team like this, you do not participate in the guessing game as other amateur investors do. Your team have a specification, and they do that job to that standard because they know exactly what to do.

Ask your refurbishment team to follow strict criteria. Measure their progress, and make sure you have check sheets for all the work required, which can be ticked off.

Always have more than one team; the number one in the property business is a very dangerous number.

Unfortunately some refurbishment teams can become complacent and expensive over time. By having more than one builder or refurbishment team you are able to rotate the teams, and typically I find this works in a cycle of threes. For example: for one project use refurbishment team 1, for the second use refurbishment team 2, for the third use refurbishment team 3, and when you get to your fourth project, revert back to refurbishment team 1.

MAKE A PLAN AND STICK TO IT

It is critical you work to a project time line, and are aware of every part of the process. This will help you stay on track throughout the refurbishment, and it gives you clarity and focus on the refurbishment. In the free downloadable workbook you will see an example of a project time line that we use in our property business. Before acquisition, you should know exactly what needs to be done, and know exactly how much it is going to cost.

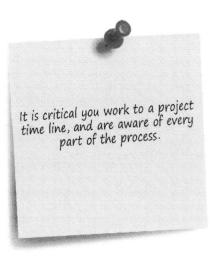

It is critical you work to a project time line, and are aware of every part of the process.

You will know exactly how long it is going to take as you have discussed it with your builder. The plan is something that will completely change your approach to the refurbishment and conversion process.

This is because by having a plan, you will be crystal clear on when you can begin to market your property so that your property can be tenanted. Also, by having a plan, you know where you stand.

A schedule will keep you organised, and if you work to the schedule, there will be no room for error. This means you work faster, and you get tasks completed as you know exactly what you have to do by the timescale you have to complete it by.

By working to a schedule, you will know if you are falling behind. The schedule will allow you to see where you actually are, and if you are behind slightly, you are able to acknowledge this and do something about it.

This may mean you hire an extra builder or decorator, or perhaps you order the supplies further in advance so that your team have supplies ready to complete the next task in your property. By doing this, it allows you and your team to accelerate where you may have been procrastinating, therefore tasks are completed faster.

To add to the idea of falling behind, if you are slightly behind schedule know why you are off schedule. This is important as it allows you to learn and grow as a property investor, because then you can improve on your next property. If you do not discover why you fell behind, this means you will make the same mistakes again and lose time.

Another major mistake people make when it comes to the plan is that they keep extending the deadline. The deadline is there for a reason, and it is imperative that you complete the refurbishment-conversion process on or preferably before the deadline.

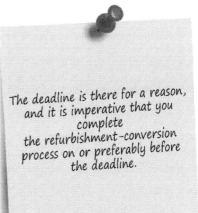

The deadline is there for a reason, and it is imperative that you complete the refurbishment-conversion process on or preferably before the deadline.

When people extend the deadline, they are letting themselves relax. In property, when it comes to any part of the process before you receive your residual income, there is no time to relax, as this will ultimately cause you to lose a lot of money. So make sure you make a plan, implement the plan, and stay in line with plan.

MAKE A BUDGET AND STICK TO IT

The last mistake that you must avoid when it comes to the refurbishment-conversion process is the temptation to overspend. Many people overspend on the refurbishment-conversion process, and therefore have an increased capital expenditure. This means they will have fewer funds available for their next project.

Once you have made your plan, you need to know exactly how much it will cost. In your budget please also include labour costs, not just the cost for the items. The reason you need to have a budget is because, like the plan, it keeps you on track. It also stops emotional decisions from being made, or decisions that are your opinion.

For example, in a general refurbishment that my teams do for me, the specification is the same all of the time, and it gets us the same, long term, sustainable and predictable results each time. So we have the roughly the same specifications for fittings and the same colour schemes which allows the refurbishment process to be systemised.

However, when you refurbish your own house, there is a lot of emotion involved, and this is completely different to the investment approach I have shared with you here. The budget stops the temptation, and there has been a clear theme in this section about saving money. When it comes to investment properties to boost your pension and income, you want to remove as much temptation as possible.

KEY LEARNINGS

1. Our definition of conversion consists of small non-structural changes which will pay for themselves by the increased return on investment over a period of three years.

2. A refurbishment and conversion adds value to a property.

3. Always stay emotionally detached when it comes to the refurbishment-conversion part of the process for your investment property.

4. Always keep a strict budget when refurbishing or converting your property.

5. Always keep a strict project time line to refer to.

6. Make note of any mistakes along the way, so that you can learn from them and improve your process.

7. Before you begin your refurbishment, select the correct team for the process.

8. When you carry out a refurbishment, factor in easy maintenance for the longer term.

WORKBOOK

For your convenience, I have put all the exercises into an easy-to-download and easy-to-print PDF workbook because it's better than writing in this book.

You can download your workbook here:
www.PremierPortfolioBuilder.co.uk/workbook

CHAPTER 5

TENANTING PROPERTY

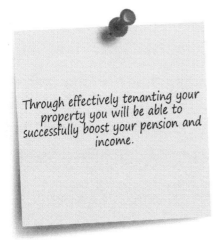

Through effectively tenanting your property you will be able to successfully boost your pension and income.

Through effectively tenanting your property you will be able to successfully boost your pension and income. Your property is a liability until you have a tenant paying you rent on a monthly basis; only then is your investment property an asset.

I find so many people who acquire property and spend huge amounts of capital on a refurbishment, only to eventually go on and select the wrong tenant for their property. These investors do not follow up on late or non-paying tenants, because they don't have the correct systems in place and are simply too busy to deal with rental arrears.

Usually these investors then find it difficult to evict such a tenant, and it can take them many months. Eventually when they do manage to remove the tenant, they find that their beautifully presented property is now in a complete and utter mess.

The following sections of this book will help you find the right tenant, manage them correctly, and avoid any major disasters.

KAM DOVEDI

If you have the right tenant it means that your rental income will be secured. Therefore, your pension will also be secure, and this is can become your route to financial freedom.

PROFILING TENANTS

Before you consider a tenant for your property, it is very important that you know which characteristics a person must have to be the type of tenant you are looking for.

The area in which you are investing, and the type of strategy you are implementing, will help you decide the correct tenant profile. If you are like me you want a tenant in your property who stays there for a long period of time, continuously pays rent on time and ultimately treats your investment property like their home.

In order to systemise and organise this process effectively, my team and I use a tenant profile check sheet. This check sheet includes all the criteria the tenant must meet in order for them to live in one of our investment properties, whether it be my property, or one of our client's investment properties. Please note that tenant profiles will vary from area to area, and from property strategy to property strategy.

We discovered earlier on that the single let strategy is the best strategy for safe, long term sustainable income. Therefore we are focusing on tried, tested and predictable property investment strategy, and I have found that the best results are achieved when renting to a single family unit.

A tenant profile check sheet allows you to remain focused, disciplined and emotionally detached when finding the correct tenant for your property. In the next section we will focus on what to consider when creating a tenant profile.

You will find a copy of the tenant check sheet we use in the free workbook which you can download online from the following link: www.PremierPortfolioBuilder.co.uk/workbook

DEMOGRAPHICS

Demographics identify the typical characteristics of your tenants. These characteristics include the age of children, annual income, education, occupation and number of individuals in their households.

Once you know your ideal tenants' demographical information, you become very clear about the correct tenant profile for your property. As soon as you know this, you will no longer have to waste time with the wrong types of tenants. When researching your demographics for your ideal tenant, please make sure you use credible sources which have used large amounts of sample data. The more reputable the source, the better and more accurate your tenant profile will be.

However, just researching the demographics is not enough when it comes to building your tenant profile. It is important you walk around your chosen investment area, and get a feel for the type of people living there. Visit the area at different times during the day, and at different times during the week. You can simply drive or walk through the streets. This task is very time consuming, but will allow you to gain a real understanding of the type of tenants in your area. Over time, you will transform your demographics research from concept to reality.

Due to the fact my team and I know our investment area thoroughly, it has allowed us to create safe, sustainable and long term property portfolios for ourselves and our clients. However, when you find your investment area, it may not be the type of area you would like to live yourself.

However, the people in that area would love to be a long term tenant in one of your properties, and this is what really counts. You want there to be a desire for tenants to live in your chosen investment area, and this desire is what makes your rental income long term.

PSYCHOGRAPHICS

You can now niche your tenant profile further with psychographics.

It is so important you are completely aware of the personality, values, opinions, attitudes, interests, and lifestyles of your prospective tenants.

As soon as you are able to master the technique of being able to match your investment properties to the tenants who desire and would love to live there, you will achieve three outstanding results:

First of all, you will be able to rent your property very quickly due to the huge demand for your investment property. Imagine renting your property within days of completing your refurbishment, or even possibly days before!

Secondly, you will be able to achieve a potential rent which may be higher than the average market rent in your area, so not only will you be earning a rental income, your rental income will be greater than other investors in your area.

Thirdly, your rental income will be long term, as the tenant you have in your investment property will want to live there for a long period of time.

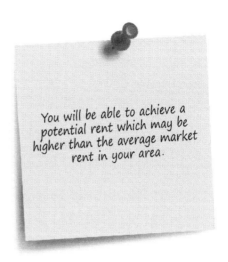

You will be able to achieve a potential rent which may be higher than the average market rent in your area.

There are three under the radar methods that you need to use in order to discover the psychographics of tenants in your area to build the correct tenant profile.

The first under the radar method is to go and speak to at least three letting agents in your chosen investment area. If you let them know you want to invest in property, they will be able to guide you to create the correct tenant profile through sharing with you the correct psychographics.

The second under the radar method is to check online lettings platforms, and observe how long it takes for a property to be rented. Once you know this timescale, follow up with a phone call to the letting agents, explaining that you are a prospective landlord and that you would like to know what type of tenants took up the tenancy.

As soon as you receive this information, create a spreadsheet for this so you can remain organised and also so that you can track and measure the data over a three to six month period in order to create the correct tenant profile.

The third under the radar method is to check online data for the socioeconomic groups in your chosen investment area.

This will help you build a realistic picture of what type of prospective tenants there are for your investment property.

The purpose of looking at a socioeconomic group is very important, as it will measure a person's work experience and an individual's or family's economic and social position in relation to others, based on income, education, and occupation.

If you show your property to tenants with the wrong psychographic, it means they will not be interested, and not decide to live in your property. Not only have you wasted precious time, you have also lost the potential income which you could have gained from renting your property quickly. The reason it takes amateur investors and accidental landlords a long period of time to rent their property is because they don't understand how important psychographics are, and therefore they don't use them.

If you show your investment property to a tenant with the right psychographic, your property will be their dream come true. Not only will they pay you rent, they will praise you for giving them such a beautiful home.

My team would only advertise to the correct psychographic for our investment area. This means the amount of time and cost involved is heavily reduced. This is because we do not waste time showing non-prospective tenants around, we are not forced to drop rents, and more importantly we do not have to negotiate and accept additional tenant demands.

However, an average landlord does, because they want to rent their property quickly and will accept anything, regardless of the consequences.

You will find the socioeconomic groups in the free workbook which you can download online from the following link: www.PremierPortfolioBuilder.co.uk/workbook

REFERENCES

The process of referencing your tenants is an essential part of being able correctly tenant your property. This will act as an indication to whether your prospective tenant will be a good tenant (i.e. someone who pays on time continuously, someone who you can charge the correct rent you desire, and someone who will remain in your property for an adequate time period which can be many years), or a bad tenant (someone who defaults on paying you rent, someone who tries to always haggle and negotiate on the rent you are charging, and someone who leaves after living in your property for a few months).

The process you follow in order to reference your tenant will hugely vary depending on your demographic and psychographic of your tenant, and there are two key approaches to referencing.

The first approach is for referencing a professional tenant. The key information you will consider is their personal credit file, employer references, and their track record for paying any previous rent. References with a current landlord and references with the landlord prior to that are also great indicators of the quality of tenant.

The prior landlord reference is usually the better indicator, as in some cases the current landlord may give a good reference to a bad tenant in order to move them on.

As well as their financial information, you also need to

look at their overall persona. For example, how do they conduct themselves? Do they provide information quickly and completely as requested? Is their manner in general pleasing, or are there any serious concerns? They are some of the behaviour signals to monitor when looking at a prospective tenant.

The second approach is for a social housing tenant who is receiving benefits from the government. The type of information required for referencing during this approach is different to that of a professional tenant.

There are many people out there who talk about referencing a 'benefits' tenant. There are other people who think they know how to reference a benefits tenant correctly. However, there are only a handful of people who really know how to make referencing work when it comes to social housing sector tenants. Please consider that this type of tenant may have social and financial challenges therefore the referencing will be very different compared to a professional.

There are four factors you must consider when referencing this type of tenant:

Firstly we make sure they have a guarantor. This could be a friend, colleague or family member of the tenant. In some cases it can be the local council, but you will need to research this yourself in order to find out.

An excellent under the radar way of learning about how the council's social housing department works is by attending their quarterly or biannual meetings for private social housing landlords.

These are generally organised by most local councils. By attending these events, you will find information and meet and build rapport with the staff who manage social housing on a day to day basis.

The second factor to make sure of is that there is an upfront deposit either in the form of a deposit guarantee from the council or from the tenant. This allows you to gain an insight into the reasons why the tenant wants to live in your property. If they do this with no questions asked, you know that they are most likely committed to living in your property for a long period of time.

Thirdly, we assess the tenant through interviewing them. The purpose of this interview for you is to assess and mitigate any risks or uncertainties associated with the tenant during this interview. One of the questions you may address is the reasons and motivations for the tenant to move into your investment property.

For example, are they requesting to live in your investment property because they have been evicted from the last property? Or is it a due to the fact that the previous landlord may have decided to sell the property the tenant was living in, so the tenant had no choice but to move?

Furthermore, being able to have a conversation with this tenant while respecting the situation that they may be in will allow you to gain insight to whether they are an ideal tenant for your property.

For example, is the tenant a single mother who life has knocked around, and is someone who simply wants a place to settle down where she can live a good life with her three young children in a place they can call home?

Or are the prospective tenants a couple of young lads, who are looking to move into a place where they can bring many of their friends along to, have no responsibilities, have no intention of settling down, and are not really house proud either? Also, because these "young lads" are not working, they spend most of the time in your property, creating extra wear and tear because they may have antisocial behaviour issues.

It is your choice when it comes to choosing they type of tenant you would like in your property.

The last factor you can check is that you can visit their current residence and assess how they are living. Is the place well looked after or is it a complete mess? All of this information helps you to assess the potential tenant and decide whether you would like them in your property.

Of course we are generalising here – each tenant needs to be vetted on their own merits, and the above are simplistic examples to demonstrate the point of vetting your tenant carefully.

Now this may seem extreme and time consuming, but remember, because they will probably not have a credit file it is very relevant to assess this as they are not working. Also they may have their own personal social challenges, and by carrying out these checks you can find an excellent tenant.

ACQUIRING TENANTS

So now you know what type of tenant to look for, what pond do you need to fish in so that you can capture these tenants, or what strategies can you implement to acquire these tenants?

WHERE TO ACQUIRE THE RIGHT TENANT

Letting Agent

This is a fantastic place to find and acquire tenants for your property. A good letting agent will find the correct tenant

A good letting agent will find the correct tenant for your property, and can also help you manage your property on an ongoing basis.

for your property, and can also help you manage your property on an ongoing basis. A good letting agent will manage any maintenance requirements as well as any mandatory compliance, for example gas safety checks, for you. Furthermore they will also make sure your investment property is being looked after by the tenant as they will carry out regular visits and checks.

For this type of service, the letting agent will usually charge a monthly fee of 10% to 12% per month, and will only deduct this from the rent you receive.

Using a letting agent to acquire the right tenant means you have a massive time saving, and you know the letting agent will do a fantastic job as they are the expert and professional in this field as it is what they do on a day-to-day basis.

Not only will this save huge amounts of your time, there will be a cost saving in terms of lower voids for your property. All the tedious and time consuming costly processes such as referencing checks, tenant profiling and viewings for your property will be carried out by the letting agent.

A good letting agent means your property investment after tenanting becomes passive, and you receive your rent, on time, continuously and hassle free.

Therefore, the ability for you to find a good letting agent is very important. I have outlined two strategies you can use in order to find a good letting agent in your chosen investment area.

The first strategy you need to use in order to find a good letting agent is the recommendations strategy. Recommendations are key for any business, and if someone gives you positive feedback on a service, they must be good at what they do.

You can get these recommendations from other property investors by attending regular property networking events, like The Premier Property Networking Club.

You can get these recommendations from other property investors by attending regular property networking events, like The Premier Property Networking Club.

Also, you can attend landlord meetings hosted by the council. The advantage of recommendations is that it means that the service that they are offering has already been tried and tested by someone else. Therefore there must be a system in place that is allowing them to achieve successful results for the property investors that they work with.

The second strategy you can use to find a good letting agent is to go and interview them. There are five specific pieces of information you must gather, and you collate this information by observing the letting agent's behaviour. This information will allow you to compare and assess letting agents once you have interviewed them.

The first piece of information you want to collect is how organised the letting agent is. The first activity you carry out in order to discover whether the letting agent is organised is to call them. For example, when you call them do they answer the phone immediately or does the phone ring continuously and divert to answer machine?

The second activity you need to carry out is to walk into their office. When you walk in, scan around the office – this acts as a huge indication as to how good their organisational skills are. For example is everything in an orderly manner, desks neat and tidy, files in their place, or are there files all over the place and circular coffee stains on the desks in the office? This is an under the radar way of assessing a letting agent's organisational skills. The next activity you carry out is to ask them to view a property as a tenant. This means that they will have to go and find a set of keys for the property. So when they go to reach for the keys, do they simply find the correctly labelled key, or are they scrambling around in the top drawer of their desk? A couple of things for you to consider.

The thing to consider is if the letting agency consists of a team, or is it a 'one man band'? In property, at any stage of the process you most definitely want a team. Imagine if an issue occurred with your property, and the only person in the office is ill or away.

This would leave you in a dire situation, where you have no one to turn to. Whereas a team means they can continue to function as normal, regardless if anyone is on holiday or ill. The number one is a dangerous number in property, so scale as soon as you can.

Thirdly, is the owner of the letting agent a property investor too, just like me and just like you? The beauty of discovering if this is the case is that this type of letting agent will look at your property from a completely different angle compared to normal letting agents; the angle of a property investor.

As well as having a unique view point, they will know all the little nuances, tips and ideas to implement to let your property even more effectively. This is why this piece of information is important to know.

The next piece of information to collect is to know if they are registered with any regulatory bodies. This is important, as it makes sure they are not going share your information, and will also make sure they have a certain amount of insurance and standards in place already, which has allowed them to become registered with regulatory bodies.

Some bodies to look at are: ARLA, (The Association of Residential Letting Agents) which is a professional body for individuals working in residential property lettings and management, Landlord accreditation schemes, ICO (Information Commissioner's Office) for data protection and The NLA (National Landlord's Association).

The last piece of information which is beneficial to check is how long they have been established. Furthermore, in the timescale they have been established, have the results they have achieved been consistently improving?

Because if they can show consistency over a period of time, it shows their systems and teams are also consistently improving, which is important for you because you are looking for a long term and sustainable income.

If they can show consistency over a period of time, it shows their systems and teams are also consistently improving, which is important for you because you are looking for a long term and sustainable income.

Local Authority

Many local authorities have an enormous need for the private sector to provide social housing. They simply do not have the resources to supply the accommodation that is required in their area, and are reliant upon private landlords for help.

Many local authorities have huge waiting lists for rented accommodation. This works to your advantage because it means your local authority can be an excellent provider of tenants for you.

There are schemes and financial benefits in certain areas for providing accommodation. They can vary considerably, therefore you will benefit from researching your chosen investment area for these.

A huge waiting list means that you have a large number of potential tenants for you to choose from. If you vet these tenants carefully, they can become excellent long term tenants, with almost a guaranteed payment structure, as the government is paying you the rent, whether it is directly or through the tenant's related benefit.

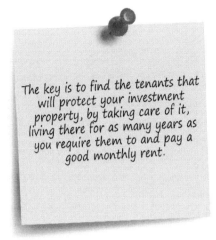

The key is to find the tenants that will protect your investment property, by taking care of it, living there for as many years as you require them to and pay a good monthly rent.

The key is to find the tenants that will protect your investment property, by taking care of it, living there for as many years as you require them to and paying a good monthly rent which you agree with them.

You must be careful when identifying whether to take on a local authority tenant, because there will generally be tenants in two types of scenarios. The first scenario is that the tenant profile shows that this tenant has been on benefits for a number of years, and the probability of them becoming employed full time is low.

This means that there is a stronger chance you will receive a regular monthly rent from this tenant.

The second scenario: if the tenant profile of the tenant shows that they have a track record of dipping in and out of employment, this is a cause for concern. This is because firstly, they will be on and off of benefits, which may result in your rental payment becoming irregular.

Also the fact that they are having short bursts of employment may also suggest that this is not a type of tenant who will provide you a long term, sustainable income. Therefore over time this will cause you a lot of frustration, which is something that you most definitely do not want, as you want this part of the process to be as hassle free as possible.

So the key is to either acquire a tenant who is in complete full time employment, or acquire a tenant from the local authority who is on benefits for the long term. This will help you create a constant passive income from the rent received.

Tenants from local authorities can be your best tenants. As long as they are the correct tenant profile, the payment is assured either through local authority, or by other means such as regular rent collecting systems you have created, this is great for you.

There a few systems that you can use; for example setting up a standing order direct from the tenant to you. Another system you can use is by making an agreement to collect the rent in cash on a specified date.

It is paramount your tenant keeps to any agreement made, and you follow up regularly if there is a delay. If you find this difficult you will find letting agents excellent to manage your property and collect rent for you. Another way to assure regular payment is to use a credit union account.

The account will belong to your local authority tenant, and the amount of money for the rent is 'ring fenced' through a credit union. This means the rent is paid to the tenant into an account, however the rent is paid out immediately to the landlord from monies coming into the account, reducing the chances for rent arrears.

Self-Marketing

Another way to acquire your tenant is by doing it yourself. This should not be your preferred route if you are starting

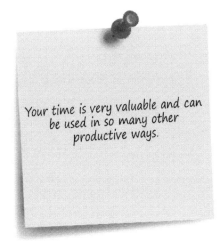

Your time is very valuable and can be used in so many other productive ways.

or have a small portfolio. This method can be very time intensive – it can be difficult without experience, and you can actually lose potential rent by longer voids as it may take you longer to find the correct tenants because you will not be familiar with the systems and processes required to become a successful letting agent. Your time is very valuable and can be used in so many other productive ways.

However if you have a portfolio of 30 or more properties this can start to become a viable option for you. You are actually becoming an 'in-house' letting agent. Some fantastic ways of acquiring tenants can be by using various online marketing platforms, such as Rightmove.co.uk, Zoopla.co.uk, and private landlord-based platforms such as UPAD, where you can market for a prospective tenant for a small cost.

Online advertisers such as Gumtree.co.uk and Vivastreet.co.uk are another great way for advertising for tenants cost effectively.

Offline methods include local newspaper ads and postcard adverts in local shops.

With local newspapers you are able to make it cost effective if you find out when the deadline for the newspaper to be published is, and you can then negotiate your ad at a lower cost if there are empty spaces in the newspaper.

You can also advertise in the classifieds section, with a very small two-line advert making the ad very cheap. Repeat the ad two or three times in the same section, so the potential for someone to call you increases.

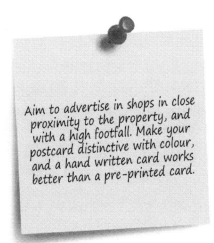

Aim to advertise in shops in close proximity to the property, and with a high footfall. Make your postcard distinctive with colour, and a hand written card works better than a pre-printed card.

Another offline strategy is to place postcards in local shop windows, and this type of self-marketing is very inexpensive. Aim to advertise in shops in close proximity to the property, and with a high footfall. Make your postcard distinctive with colour, and a hand written card works better than a pre-printed card.

MANAGING TENANTS

This is the most crucial part of your property portfolio. This is where your income from property truly becomes passive if done correctly. If not, your property portfolio will turn in to a bottomless, money-swallowing pit.

This is the most crucial part of your property portfolio.

Bad paying tenants lead to maintenance issues, maintenance issues lead to the tenants leaving, and tenants leaving means that you now have a liability on your hands rather than an asset. You must make sure that there are systems, processes and procedures in effect so that both the rent collection and maintenance part of the tenanting is always up to date.

LETTING AGENT

Although I shared this with you earlier, the first way to manage tenants in your investment property is through a good letting agent. This is an excellent way of managing your tenants and not having to be involved in the day-to-day management of tenants that is required during lettings.

A good letting agent will manage your property portfolio and therefore make your property portfolio a completely passive investment for you.

A good letting agent will manage your property portfolio and therefore make your property portfolio a completely passive investment for you. This allows you to concentrate on other aspects of your life, whether it is your property business, your full time career, or your family and fulfilling your passions and dreams.

The fact that you are not involved in the tenanting part of the property process results in you having choices. For a letting agent to manage your property and tenants to the best possible standard, there are a number of criteria they need to meet.

Firstly they need to have excellent systems, processes and procedures in place as this will make your life so much easier.

Here are a few examples of the systems good letting agents use:

CFP WINMAN; this is letting agents' management software, and is used by letting agents managing 100 or more properties. Many large independent letting agent companies have this package due to the scale they have to manage.

JAKX is another letting agents' management software which gives similar results to CFP WINMAN, and is a competitor.

Larger corporate letting agents will have their own bespoke software systems in place.

Independent letting agents will use packages such as Landlord and Letting Agents Manager by Portfolio Software. This software can be used by landlords who decide to carry out the lettings process themselves, as it makes the lettings side of the property process clear and focused.

To know a letting agent is using these types of management software gives you confidence that they are capable of managing your property well.

As well as knowing of the systems used by the letting agents for the management of your property, it is important you check what processes your letting agents have for acquiring tenants, managing tenants' viewings and referencing tenants too.

You can find this out by simply asking them what they have in place, and as you are a prospective customer they should be forthcoming with this information, so you can make an informed decision about whether to use their services.

These processes and procedures will vary, although there is no need to understand the complete details unless you are considering starting a letting agents yourself.

When you are starting, knowing there is combination of spread sheets, daily task sheets, project management software, and CRM (customer relationship management systems) is a key criteria and is enough to put your faith in a letting agent.

Even though systems are great in a business, human interaction between colleagues and clients is also very important during management.

Clear communication within the letting agents, complete organisation between their team, with tenants, and you is essential. It makes good sense to pay a good letting agent well that has all of these aspects in their management service.

Clear communication within the letting agents, complete organisation between their team, with tenants, and you is essential.

SELF-MANAGED

On the other hand, you may choose to self-manage your property if you are making this your full time career.

Self-management works well if you have a sizeable

property portfolio of 30 or more properties as a minimum. This allows you to build a team for property management.

As a guide, on average a person working for you in full time employment is able to manage up to 50 properties.

I personally would definitely not recommend this approach if you are just starting or have a small portfolio. Your time is best suited to other parts of your property career and you will very much benefit from leveraging the services of a good letting agent.

Five to seven properties can provide you a pension or a boost in income which equates to the national average net income achieved by someone in full time employment.

On average five to seven properties can provide you a pension or a boost in income which equates to the national average net income achieved by someone in full time employment. Even though this is a generalisation, and everyone has their own goals, you do not have to be managing your own properties to become financially free.

BEST PRACTICES

During the lettings part of the process, there are certain best practices that you must follow in order to build and maintain a strong relationship with both tenants and letting agents.

So let's look at the tenant first. For you to build a strong relationship with a tenant, the first objective you must complete is to provide them with a clean, tidy, and presentable property.

The number of investors I have met who do not clean their property before tenanting is unbelievable. This is why they have long void periods, and when they find the tenant, they have no reason to keep your property clean, as it was never clean when it was originally presented to them.

The next objective you must complete for your tenant if you would like to be head and shoulders above any other landlord is to provide them with a welcome pack. This is a simple document with contact numbers, local amenities, guarantees, and public transport details. Accompanied with the document you could provide a hamper comprising of some tea, coffee, and biscuits. If you do this, you will have a tenant who will love you and your property, and will most likely remain there for a very long time, as no other landlord would have treated them in this way. A small percentage of landlords do this, which is why they have the best tenants.

Now you have discovered how to build a strong relationship with a tenant, here is how to build a strong relationship with a letting agent.

The first way is to monitor the performance of your letting agent and schedule quarterly meetings with them to make sure that everything is on track. These meetings can be either a 10-minute conversation over the telephone, or a 15-minute meeting at their offices.

This will help your letting agent know that you are a proactive landlord, without coming across as pushy or arrogant.

Furthermore, it also helps you keep in their mind space which helps you to build an even stronger rapport and allow them to continue to do a great job for you.

When building relationships, you must also know the long term implications, for example, when signing agreements with letting agents, always check the penalties in place for ending their service should you choose to. Also, always check and confirm any additional costs you may have to pay for any other services.

When signing agreements with letting agents, always check the penalties there are for ending their service should you choose to.

KEY LEARNINGS

1. Your investment property is only an asset once it has been rented.

2. Create a tenant profile before you consider renting your investment property.

3. A tenant profile consists of demographics, psychographics and references.

4. Always research the area thoroughly to make sure you have identified the correct tenant profile.

5. When researching, use credible and reputable sources who have reached a summary of data using large and relevant data samples.

6. A letting agent saves you both time and money.

7. Make sure your letting agent is regulated.

8. One of the best ways to find a tenant is from the local housing authority, as there is a waiting list of tenants who require housing.

9. Build a relationship with the tenant and the letting agent.

WORKBOOK

For your convenience, I have put all the exercises into an easy-to-download and easy-to-print PDF workbook because it's better than writing in this book.

You can download your workbook here:
www.PremierPortfolioBuilder.co.uk/workbook

CHAPTER 6

THREE APPROACHES TO BUILDING A SUCCESSFUL PROPERTY PORTFOLIO

You have reached the point in this book where you now understand how property is the vehicle that will really allow you to have a long term and sustainable passive income. This will allow you to boost your pension and your income.

You have also discovered that the single let strategy is a fantastic strategy to implement, and you now know that in order to become a successful property investor you must have a system, like the ACT Formula, and a winning team.

I focused on key aspects within the ACT Formula, so that you were able to gain an insight into the knowledge needed to make your property investing a success.

In this chapter, you will learn the different approaches you have in order to build your own property portfolio, and the advantages and disadvantages of each approach. This way you can choose the approach that is best suited for you.

DO IT YOURSELF (DIY)

The first approach you can take is the do it yourself approach.

The advantages are that first of all, you are your own boss, you can make all of the decisions.

The second advantage is that you accurately know the costs of each product and service you purchase, down to the last penny. You are able to calculate exactly what something will cost because you know all the figures within the complete property process.

The next advantage is that you will know all of the processes involved when it comes to property investment. In fact you are so involved in the process that you actually become part of the process. Therefore, ultimately you are responsible, and you don't need to rely on anyone else.

The ACT Formula, a great framework.

I have shared with you the ACT Formula, a great framework and as much practical information as I could get in to this book for you.

The do it yourself approach is great if you are a full time investor or can spend a considerable amount of time in property.

You, on the other hand, now recognise that property is

hard work, and it does involve a lot of time, effort and resources if you want to make it a success.

Property is statistically proven to be the most expensive asset we buy in our lifetimes, yet people take huge risks and 'dabble', while in any other profession we go straight to the experts.

For example, if your car breaks down, you don't rip out the engine and try to find out what it wrong with it, you take it to the professional which is the mechanic.

In property there is no money back guarantee on a property; once it has been signed, sealed and delivered, that is it.

Any mistakes in property can be very expensive, and it can take you many years of your time, effort and resources to overcome those mistakes.

The disadvantages do out-weigh the advantages in the case of the DIY approach.

The first main disadvantage is that you will play too small because you are doing everything yourself. The fact that you are doing everything means that you will not have the time to expand your property business.

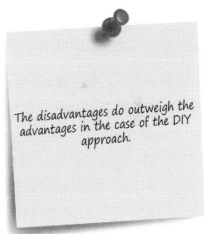

The disadvantages do outweigh the advantages in the case of the DIY approach.

You will lose very good property opportunities because

you will be too busy. This means you will lose thousands and thousands of pounds because of the fact you are doing everything in the property process, and over many years it can equate to the loss of millions of pounds.

The next disadvantage is the fact that you will have lose a huge amount of time, and this time could be spent somewhere else. The time you spend researching, acquiring, converting and tenanting is time that you can never get back. The time lost through making mistakes is also something that you can never get back.

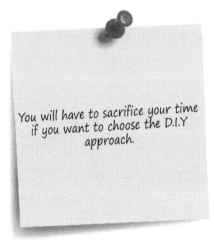

You will have to sacrifice your time if you want to choose the DIY approach.

You will have to sacrifice your time if you want to choose the DIY approach.

This means less time to see your family, less time to show interest in your loved ones, less time to enjoy your hobbies, and less time to have the chance to fulfil your passions.

Another disadvantage is to do with the team you have to build. In any business, you always have a core team, and these people in your core team must have the same mission as you, and must be with you each step of the way.

This team takes time to develop, as many people will come and go. Therefore to build the right core team, you will have to be prepared to go through a long period of trial and error.

I am grateful to say that my core team has remained the same for the last 22 years out of the last 25 years of my property investing journey. I am always adding very special and unique individuals to my core team.

If you would like to view the advantages and disadvantages of this approach in a table format, you will find this in the free workbook which you can download online from the following link: www.PremierPortfolioBuilder.co.uk/workbook

DONE WITH YOU (DWY)

The second approach to building a successful property portfolio is the done with you approach. In this approach, you are not doing everything yourself as you will be working with people who have knowledge and expertise in the field of property.

The done with you approach is the accelerated version of the do it yourself approach.

There are three ways to the done with you approach. The first is with a joint venture partner, and the second is through education and third is with a mentor.

JOINT VENTURE PARTNER

There is legislation around carrying out joint ventures, so please make sure you do your own due diligence and research before entering into a joint venture. There are two main advantages of a joint venture partner:

The first advantage is that they may have the funds available to invest in a project that you may not have. This allows you to carry out the project that you may not have been able to carry out otherwise.

The second advantage is that your joint venture partner may be able to offer you certain skill sets and contacts that you may not possess. For example, they may be excellent project managers, or very good at organising and structuring budgets for a project.

Also, they may have contacts who are able to do certain things that you cannot do, for example, make the process more tax efficient, have the ability to drive down costs, or even have the ability to give you advice and show you how to carry out certain property processes correctly.

Here are the three major disadvantages:

The first key disadvantage is that many people make the mistake of not finding a match between themselves and the joint venture partner first. They enter into a joint venture partnership where their goals are completely different, and this type of partnership will never last for long.

For example, if you and I were joint venture partners, the first thing I would check is to see if there was a match between us.

The discussion about returns and money will come after this initial step. I would make sure you like what my team and I do, you appreciate and buy into our vision mission and values, and ultimately that you have faith and trust in us to do the job correctly, efficiently and professionally.

Only after this will we discuss returns and capital

expenditure. Each month, I am inundated with requests to joint venture because we have a reputation for the tried, tested and predictable results we achieve and people respect my team and me, therefore they want to work with us.

The second disadvantage of a joint venture is that you are still held accountable. The joint venture partner shares responsibility, therefore you are still accountable for your part of the joint venture.

You are still accountable for your part of the joint venture.

This means that you still have to go and take action, while avoiding any mistakes that you make along the way.

The third key disadvantage is that people change, their circumstances change, their ideas and motivations change, and it can become very difficult for you if your joint venture partner decides to change their direction.

EDUCATION

The third done with you approach is through education. I have founded The Premier Property Networking Club, which is an event in Canary Wharf, London, where we have the best property professionals attend to deliver keynote speeches, and to educate delegates. This is an event purely to come and learn about property and network with like-minded people, and creating an event like The Premier

Property Networking Club is very important to me as it benefits you.

Here are the major advantages and disadvantages of the property education approach.

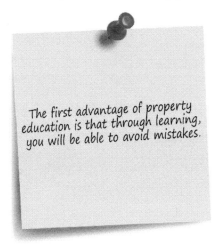

The first advantage of property education is that through learning, you will be able to avoid mistakes.

The first advantage of property education is that through learning, you will be able to avoid mistakes. This means that you will save time as well as money.

You will follow tried and tested strategies where there is a formula, blueprint or model which will fast track your success.

You will feel an urgency to succeed as you are in a positive learning environment.

The disadvantage is that firstly it can lead to someone becoming a course 'junkie'.

This means that this person will buy a course after course after course, and end up in huge amounts of debt without implementing what is learnt.

Therefore this person will be in a stage of information overload as they have learnt so many different strategies and are confused where to start, and the capital that they may have had to invest, they may have lost through paying for the courses.

The last disadvantage with courses is that the focus is on

you to implement what you have learnt, and this is where most investors fall down. Life simply gets in the way.

If you would like to view the advantages and disadvantages of this approach in a table format, you will find this in the free workbook which you can download online from the following link: www.PremierPortfolioBuilder.co.uk/workbook

MENTOR

The third aspect to this approach is working with mentors and coaches. My definition of a mentor is someone who has achieved outstanding results in property, and is someone who has already done what you want to do, and they can show you how to replicate their results using their knowledge, experience

A mentor is someone who has achieved outstanding results in property, and is someone who has already done what you want to do.

and contacts. Contrastingly, a coach is someone who can share a process or educate you, but hasn't followed the path themselves, and this is the distinction between mentors and coaches.

One of the key advantages of a mentor is that there will be some time saving and cost saving. This is because they can share with you their past mistakes, and they can help you to decide what to do and what not to do. This means that not only do you save yourself the mistakes, you save the money you would have lost by making those mistakes.

Another advantage of a property mentor is that if they are a good mentor, they will hold you accountable. This is because you are now their responsibility, and your success is important to them. I speak from experience when I say this, as I have mentored over 100 property investors, and their success is very important to me. So I will sit down with them, take their plan apart, give them a set of actions, and then expect the actions to be completed in a certain timescale, and this is exactly the same as what my mentors worth multi-million and billion pounds do with me. This accountability is what will allow you to stay focused and stay on the straight and narrow. Mistakes in property are very expensive, and a good mentor will show you how to avoid these mistakes.

Mistakes in property are very expensive, and a good mentor will show you how to avoid these mistakes.

One final key advantage is one that takes time to develop. Eventually if you implement action correctly and quickly, you will begin to get closer to the achievements of your mentor, and in some cases may actually surpass them. This is such a great feeling, to know that you have excelled past someone who was mentoring you. When this happens, you enter into their peer group level, and if your mentor is very good, this group will be full of very influential and successful people.

However it will take a lot of time before you can consider overtaking your mentor.

Now let's consider the disadvantages.

The first disadvantage is this: how do you know they are a good mentor? There are many people in the property industry who act as amazing property investors, but they have really just positioned themselves there.

The second disadvantage is that even though you are held accountable, it is still up to you to complete the actions that have been set. As a mentor I am very careful who to mentor, and there is a strict vetting process before I work with people. I give and expect 110% from my mentees, and for the dedicated person, their success is guaranteed.

The last disadvantage is that if the mentor you are working with is successful, their time will be very important. Therefore it will be very costly for you. I have many different mentors, in property and business, and in some cases I am paying tens of thousands of pounds for just 120 minutes of time. In some cases I have paid thousands of pounds for only a 15-minute mentoring session! Crazy right? But this has allowed me to accelerate very quickly over the years and I actively seek mentors who are the best of the best. I know their time has a monetary value, and am happy to pay this. As a mentor myself I keep to the same values I install in my mentees. That is to work out their monetary value on their time. So my time is very expensive, which is why I only work with committed individuals. The question we need to ask ourselves is what is expensive or costly to us? Because if you receive an excellent return on your investment by achieving fantastic results, surely the cost becomes irrelevant.

DONE FOR YOU (DFY)

The third and final approach is the done for you approach.

In this approach you achieve fast results by allowing a property portfolio building company like us to carry out the complete process for you.

I am the founder of Premier Portfolio Builder, the fastest-growing property portfolio building company in the south east of England.

We offer a bespoke service that is tailored to you, and you can acquire just one property or many.

"Premier Portfolio Builder is a Property Portfolio Building service, where we carry out the complete property process for our investors. We manage all the aspects of the process, from purchase through to refurbishment and then ongoing lettings and management."

You can find out more at www.PremierPortfolioBuilder. co.uk

So now let's evaluate the advantages and disadvantages of using a property portfolio building company.

The first advantage of a property portfolio building company like us is that there is zero procrastination. From the moment you are ready to begin, systems, processes

The first advantage of a Property Portfolio building company like us is that there is zero procrastination.

and procedures are implemented correctly, and because of this you benefit from excellent results.

The second advantage is the speed at which the results are achieved. The done for you approach is the most accelerated approach out of the three approaches.

There is no delay between stages in the property process, and the property investing journey becomes a very easy and a hassle free process for you.

There is a clear tried and tested system in place.

Another advantage of the done for you approach is that there is a clear tried and tested system in place and many investors and in our case the founder, myself, have used these systems to get ahead in property.

There are cost savings throughout for you due to the economies of scales, i.e. there is a clear process repeated many times using the same teams and same products. This allows the costs to be driven down. These cost savings, time savings, and efficiency savings are all passed to you.

The service a property portfolio building company offers means that your time involvement is minimal.

There is no need for you to go and research the area, go and source the correct properties, go and find quotations for a refurbishment, carry out the refurbishment, or find the correct letting agents.

This means that you save huge amounts of time. This means that you can concentrate on your career, with the peace of mind knowing your financial future is being built safely and securely.

The time saving means you can spend more time with your friends and family.

You have the chance to enjoy your favourite pastimes and hobbies. The ability to save your own time gives you many more choices.

The time saving means you can spend more time with your friends and family.

However, even though the time involvement is minimal, the key decisions are still yours. For example when it comes the property acquisition, and a potential property is found, you can choose whether you want to purchase that property or not – the decision is always yours.

Furthermore, even though the key decisions are yours, the portfolio building company is accountable to you and they have to answer to you.

The main advantage is that this is a completely passive investment.

You are not involved in the tedious and time consuming day-to-day processes, which results in you having the peace of mind that you know everything is being implemented for you in the most cost effective, long term and efficient way.

The main disadvantage with this approach is that there may be a small upfront fee, but a good property portfolio building company will make sure that these costs are 100% absorbed into the cost savings for the whole process. So in real terms you are actually saving money, time and mistakes.

The other main disadvantage is finding the correct property portfolio building service for you.

So now you have discovered the done for you approach with a property portfolio building company like us, here is what you should you look for in a property portfolio building company to know that they are excellent.

If you would like to view the advantages and disadvantages of this approach in a table format, you will find this in the free workbook which you can download online from the following link: www.PremierPortfolioBuilder.co.uk/workbook

THE KEY CRITERIA YOU SHOULD ASSESS FOR A PROPERTY PORTFOLIO BUILDING COMPANY

Firstly, where are they are investing in the UK?

You must make sure that they are investing a real hot spot, and an area which has a very high growth potential.

For example, Premier Portfolio Builder invests in the Greater London urban area, which is just on the edge of London as I like to call it. From Savills research, the growth forecast in the south east of England is the highest amongst any other region in the UK. We are investing so close to London, only 30 minutes by train, this means there will be a chance for an even higher potential capital growth. Also, the areas we are investing in are part of the largest regeneration project in Europe. These are some of the facts you must consider in order to know if the portfolio building company is investing a real hot spot.

The second aspect is how do they charge for their service?

Is it all one huge upfront fee, or can you test their service?

We offer a tailored package depending on our client's needs. You must look for a company that is not a 'sausage machine' type of company, where you fit into their standard package.

The portfolio building company should really listen to your needs very carefully and be willing to spend time with you; only then will they be able to find the correct solution for you.

There must be an action plan created that is specific for your needs and goals.

Also there should be flexibility in the portfolio building service.

Otherwise when you give someone a massive fee, it means that you are locked in with them without having tested their service.

Do they take any share in your rental income or the capital growth in your property?

There are companies out there who will build you a portfolio, but will take a massive chunk out of the income or capital growth. Something you should be aware of.

Another key criterion to consider for a good property portfolio building company is if they offer a personable service.

Check out if they actually care about you or are you just a figure on their spreadsheet.

Can you have a conversation with them where they listen to you and help you to the best of their ability? One of the great people we have worked with is Ranjit Singh Schaggar, and what he loved the most about what we do is that it was a personable service. Any other company would have just taken his money, and that was it.

The fact that our clients are able to speak to me is important to them; they can call me at any time, email me, and they will receive a response from me, not from a PA, or my marketing team, or my core team. I believe this to be important. I know I am the founder, and have multi-million pound businesses, and if I was in your position of choosing a 'done for you' service, I would feel much more comfortable if I was able to speak to the founder of the company as it would mean that they actually do care.

If I was able to speak to the founder of the company it would mean that they actually do care.

The next step is to go and view current projects.

First of all, if they can't show you current projects, then they are not delivering on what they are promising.

Second, by viewing the current projects, it makes it real for you, and makes it much more tangible. There are people who literally want to work with us so eagerly, they just want to give us the money, because of the reputation we have.

However, my team and I would always encourage you to come and view our projects, come and assess us. It makes me feel a lot more comfortable that you have seen the process, and it will make you feel much more comfortable by knowing we over deliver on everything we promise to you.

So after you have seen the projects, it is time for the facts and figures.

Can the portfolio building company show you a clear structure of the calculations for a typical investment property that they purchase?

Should you choose to work with us, and come and see us, during our meeting we will go through all of these facts and figures. All the calculations are clearly presented for you in a premier analysis document, which you can take away with you.

How transparent are they when it comes to giving information?

These figures are from a recently done property deal and totally real and current figures.

The next aspect you check is how transparent they are when it comes to giving information and discussing what they do and the model that you use.

The ability to be completely transparent with a potential client or someone who is already a client is very important. This makes you feel much more comfortable when it comes to working with us. Trust me.

The last piece of due diligence I will mention for your benefit that you must carry out on a property portfolio building company like us, before you invest with us, is to check that the results are proven.

You can do this first by reading the testimonials on a website that they may have, for example when you visit www.PremierPortfolioBuilder.co.uk there is a tab which says "success stories" which is has testimonials from some of our clients who have used our service.

Also, if they are truly confident in the service they offer, they will allow you to speak to clients who have already used their service. This way you can ask the clients any questions you choose, and they will give an unbiased answer, which is important to you. I am very grateful that we have clients who openly just tell people things like our "service is great", and that they are "so happy the found us at the right time".

Now you know all the approaches that you have, and how to find a portfolio building company that ticks all of the correct boxes, if you feel you would like to know more about what Premier Portfolio Builder can do for you, and you would like to meet us and see more, feel free to contact us on: 01634 838 745 or email us: info@ premierportfoliobuilder.co.uk

If you would like to view the key criteria for successfully choosing a property portfolio building company in a table format, you will find this in the free workbook which you can download online from the following link: www. PremierPortfolioBuilder.co.uk/workbook

KEY LEARNINGS

1. The DIY approach is a dangerous approach which will lead to you losing time and money if you are not investing as a full time career.

2. Before carrying out the done with you approach with a joint venture partner, make sure all of the terms are clear.

3. A mentor can fast track your success, and you will have to implement their guidance.

4. Property education is great, but once you have absorbed the knowledge you will then have to take action.

5. The done for you approach is for you if you have funds available but do not have the time, experience or knowledge to action the property process.

6. When choosing a property portfolio building company, always make sure that they are investing in the correct high growth area.

7. When choosing a property portfolio building company, make sure that they can answer all your questions.

8. When choosing a property portfolio building company make sure that they have a track record with clients who have used their service.

9. Asses a property portfolio building company with key criteria.

WORKBOOK

For your convenience, I have put all the exercises into an easy-to-download and easy-to-print PDF workbook because it's better than writing in this book.

You can download your workbook here:
www.PremierPortfolioBuilder.co.uk/workbook

CHAPTER 7

SUMMARY

CREATE THE LIFE OF YOUR DREAMS

Property is an asset class that increases in value over time, while at the same time providing you with a residual income. Not only is this income continuous but it is also massive. By investing in property, you are no longer trading your time for money, and over time, you will have the option if you choose to replace the income from your job. This is why property is not a get rich quick scheme; it is a medium to long term wealth creation strategy, where you will become extremely wealthy over time. This increase in wealth means that the potential value of your pension pot will increase over time also. The reason why property is better compared to other investments is because of the fact that in property, the fluctuations of property values are much less. This means that the gradual increase of values and income will allow you to tack inflation; something not a lot of investments can offer. So property is a great asset class, but how do you overcome that first step of taking action? It is simple; know your reason why you want to invest in property, as the method on how to achieve success in property becomes much easier.

WHAT YOU NEED TO KNOW TO BE A SUCCESSFUL PROPERTY INVESTOR

A successful property investor always has a winning team around them. Not only that, but a successful investor makes sure that there are multiple professionals in each position of the property process, for example multiple mortgage brokers, solicitors, etc. This is built up over time. If someone does a job better than you, let them do it; it will save you time, money and a lot of pain. To make sure your team are working efficiently, communication between you and them is very important. To save time in the future, and so that you can grow your team faster, build a system as you go along your journey. This way anyone in your team can be replaced if they leave, and anyone can be added to a certain part of the process. As well as a winning team, a successful investor must have a winning strategy. This is the single let strategy as it is the most tried and tested, and will provide you a long term residual income and future capital growth. There are many strategies out in the property market; therefore you must look carefully at the realistic figures when comparing strategies. A successful property investor must know the costs at each stage of the property process, all the way through the property process. Not only the strategy, but the area is very important; consider very carefully the capital growth and monthly income potential for the area you are investing in. Overall, to become a successful property investor takes time. Therefore you must learn patience, be able to improve on what you know, and be able to make changes when necessary. This is why knowledge is a great starting point.

ACQUIRING PROPERTY

Before you acquire any property, you must do your due diligence on an area before you buy. You are looking for an area with good infrastructure, high growth potential and an area which is close to London, ideally in the south east of England. In that area, you must make sure that the rental demand is high, as this will affect your long term income. Once you find an area, you then begin to focus on the best streets. On these streets you will find the best property investment opportunities. However, before you purchase them you must make sure that the calculations work. Always make sure the capital expenditure does not adversely affect your calculations. Always calculate the return on investment as well as yield. Now you know the area and the calculations, you will need to know the acquisition channels. The first acquisition channel is the estate agent. Remember, estate agents only like to work with preferred buyers who perform. The second acquisition channel is through auction. Auction properties may be incompletely described, so always go and visit the auction property. The third acquisition channel is the direct to vendor channel. With this strategy there is a trade-off between cost and time. Therefore the first action you must take is to become an expert in one acquisition channel and then move on to another following acquisition channel.

CONVERTING OR REFURBISHING A PROPERTY

Our definition of conversion consists of small non-structural changes which will pay for themselves by the increased return on investment over a period of three years. A refurbishment is where you make cosmetic changes to return the property back to its original condition. A refurbishment and conversion adds value to a property. Always stay emotionally detached when it comes to the refurbishment-conversion part of the process for your investment property. Always keep a strict budget when refurbishing or converting your property. This can be helped by keeping a strict project time line to refer to. Gaining experience on how to carry out a refurbishment effectively is very important. So make note of any mistakes along the way, so that you can learn from them, and improve your process. Before you begin your refurbishment, select the correct team for the process. When you carry out a refurbishment, factor in easy maintenance for the longer term.

TENANTING PROPERTY

Your investment property is only an asset once it has been rented. The first action you must take when it comes to the tenanting part of the property process is to create a tenant profile before you consider renting your investment property. A tenant profile consists of demographics, psychographics and references. Always research the area thoroughly to make sure you have identified the correct tenant profile. When researching, use credible and reputable sources who have reached a summary of data using large and relevant data samples. Once you have collated your research, there are three ways in which you can find and manage tenants. One way is through a letting agent, who will save you both time and money. Make sure your letting agent is regulated. Build a relationship with the tenant and the letting agent. Another under the radar way to find potential tenants, and possibly one of the best ways to find a tenant, is from the local housing authority, as there is a waiting list of tenants who require housing.

THE THREE APPROACHES TO BUILDING A SUCCESSFUL PROPERTY PORTFOLIO

The first approach is the do it yourself approach, and this is a dangerous approach which will lead to you losing time and money unless you are investing your time in creating your property portfolio, full time or considerably part time.

The second approach is the done with you approach. This is an accelerated approach. Working with a joint venture partner, make sure all of the terms are clear. Another way is through education, and once you have absorbed the knowledge you will then have to take action.

The final approach is the done for you approach. The done for you approach is for you if you have funds available but do not have the time, experience or knowledge to action the property process correctly. Therefore you will benefit and can choose the correct property portfolio building company to carry out this process for you.

When choosing a property portfolio building company, always make sure that they are investing in the correct high growth area, ideally near London. Also, make sure that the property portfolio building can answer all your questions. A very important factor is to check they have no equity share in your property – this is key. Check they offer a tailor made bespoke service where you can test them with just one property. And that they have a track record of clients who have used their service, they genuinely care about you and are totally transparent.

YOUR NEXT STEP

I would like to personally thank you and congratulate you for reaching this point in this book. It shows me that you are someone who wants to take their financial future into their own hands. I hope you found the content of this book to be informative, useful and practical.

I do sincerely hope you now continue your property investing journey so you too can boost your income and pension pot to the level you desire, just like the dozens of people I have worked with already.

If you would like to take control of your financial future through investing in property and simply don't have the time, experience and knowledge, then we are here to help. Email us now at: info@premierportfoliobuilder.co.uk

The next step is just to simply find out if there is a match between us and we will be happy to answer any of your questions.

Looking forward to working with you soon.

To your success,

Kam Dovedi

Founder of Premier Portfolio Builder

www.PremierPortfolioBuilder.co.uk

SUCCESS STORIES

Daniel Wagner – Seven-figure businessman

"Premier Portfolio Builder is a great hands free service, where you put in none of your own time or effort, but you get maximum results. I know the founder well and can vouch that they are personable and professional, and they deliver a great service, highly recommend it if you are looking to secure your financial future for you and your loved ones".

Petrus De Jager – Personal trainer

"I chose Premier Portfolio Builder because they are open and honest from the start, some portfolio companies ask to retain equity in your property where these guys don't, and the location is very close to London where the numbers still stack up. The benefit is that I can still work full time and invest in property that is affordable to me. It takes away the time I would spend looking and viewing properties and putting in offers, where Kam and his team have relationships with local agents which source them the right properties, almost impossible to get ourselves. I found out about Kam at a property conference weekend. I would recommend as they are there every step of the process, you can call or visit any time, there is no pressure or hard selling – the pace is set by yourself. Investing in property is a great way to leverage money, using Premier

Portfolio Builder is a great way to leverage time – it does cost you but the finances and time you save is worth it".

Ashish Garg – Commissioning engineer at BP

"We discovered 'Premier Portfolio Builder' at the Property Exhibition, Excel London. With a very limited property investment experience, myself along with my better half are always on the lookout for opportunities. We were truly inspired with Kam's presentation on how he gradually built up the property portfolio from nothing. Due to my work commitments, although I am very keen to invest in the property, I cannot afford to spend time – this is where premier portfolio plays an important role in providing a complete "hands-free" solution. Once I reflected interest, an initial meeting was arranged with Kam to assess my personal situation and objective. Very soon, I benefited from Premier's experience in discovering a hidden property gem, which will hopefully bring 'Value for Money' and prove to be a good investment. As a part of service, I was provided with information on refurbishment costs even before making the formal offer, as well as an introduction to an efficient mortgage adviser was very helpful.

Currently, I am in the process of finalising the purchase of this property. However, I have no hesitation in recommending Premier Portfolio for their excellent service and personalised support from start to finish".

Peter Nicholson – Property investor

"The reason I started using Premier Portfolio Builder rather than doing it myself is frankly because I like doing other things, like raising finance. They are out there and they have their finger on the pulse in their areas, I've done the numbers and the fee Premier Portfolio Builder charge I have more than recovered. Looking to do my next one, and that will be my third in six months, I am looking to build a sizeable portfolio".

Caroline Butson – Former corporate P.A

"Premier Portfolio Builder have taken control of my house buying, refurbishing and renting in a professional, yet always reassuringly friendly manner. With my amateur buy to rent knowledge, the only thing I knew for sure was that I wanted money coming in for as little work as possible on my part and as sure a thing as possible. Being unused to joint venturing and scared if, I'm honest, of giving someone else a chunk of money, I had possible future newspaper headlines running through my head: *"The only way she viewed the property before purchasing was via photos!" said Property Magazine.* Being rather risk adverse, I asked a lot of questions and needed lots of guidance. At no time did I feel patronised, persuaded to a course of action I didn't want to take or out of touch. They were always prompt in reply to my emails/texts/calls. It helped as they have done the process many times. If there were any queries or obstacles these were dealt with and it felt as in control as a process as it could do considering I hadn't done this type of thing before. I would recommend Premier Portfolio Builder wholeheartedly. They have taken my project from start to finish and made it a success. If I had tried to do it myself it would have taken three times as long, along with many pitfalls along the way. They know the pitfalls and have the experience to deal with anything untoward, they are unflappable".

Richard L – Film director

"I had been looking to get on the buy to let ladder for a while. A friend of mine who had already been through the Premier Portfolio Builder service introduced me to Kam from Premier Portfolio Builder. They helped me secure my first buy to let property and have done an amazing job on the refurb and sourcing... I have seen a couple of their other projects and I am extremely impressed and grateful, thank you very much".

Emily Cusack – Nurse

"I met The Premier Portfolio Builder team at a property show, and they showed me their hands free investing model. At that point I thought to myself I like the sound of that! It was really easy because I didn't have to do anything; all I had to do was sign the dotted line with the solicitors, and now I get cash flow from a property I own every month".

Tommy Franzen – Professional actor & dancer

"In the community I happened to bump into a great guy called Kam, from Premier Portfolio Builder. From the start they have been helping me build my portfolio, so they found me a property, found me a broker, building team, solicitor, everything was done for me. Here I am standing in my first house! This has been a really good and easy service, all good!"

Ranjit Singh – Professional investor

"I have to say Premier Portfolio Builder are unique. I have never felt so comfortable investing in property before, I know for a fact no other company would have helped me at the start as much as they did, and this was even before the process had actually begun. They are truly here to help as many people as they can, and the service they offer is fantastic. Really happy I got involved with them and fully recommend their service to whoever is looking to become financially free, because they will make it happen!"

Marc Nicholson – Entrepreneur

"I had been watching the founder of Premier portfolio Builder for 18 months, I saw how he helped people, and how his company were giving people excellent results. I then one day approached him and said "I have been watching you", to my amazement he didn't run away. Fast forward to now...Using Premier Portfolio Builder has been one of the best decisions I have ever made, because while I am travelling the world, or doing other hobbies, my portfolio is being built, and I am directly being paid the income from my properties. This is what you call passive! Fully recommend!"

Jean Botfield – Retired

"I heard Kam Dovedi speaking at a Property Training event earlier this year. He spoke knowledgably on what to look for in a letting agent. Coincidentally at that same event I spoke to a woman who was a client of Kam's company and she recommended them to me. She had purchased a house that Premier Portfolio Builder had sourced, arranged the refurbishment and managed for her. She was now refinancing the property to release some equity and planned to buy a further property with their help.

I was looking to purchase a buy to let property and had

recently been disappointed when a couple of properties I was purchasing fell through after I had spent time and money on valuations and solicitors fees.

I contacted Premier Portfolio Builder and arranged to meet. Kam explained how Premier Portfolio Builder Worked and we went to view some of the properties in the area that they had recently acquired for clients so I could see for myself the type of property and see examples of the refurbishment.

Very quickly Premier Portfolio Builder sourced a property for me. I used the Mortgage Brokers and Solicitors they (work with) recommended. The whole process has gone very smoothly. Currently my property is being worked on by Kam's team and doing a great job.

The property will be ready to rent by the end of this month and Premier Portfolio Builder will manage the property for me. I am hoping to refinance within six months to a year to pull out the majority of my deposit.

For armchair investors who don't have the time or inclination to find a suitable property, sort out the various trades to do the refurbishment and then find a good letting agent Premier Portfolio Builder offers an excellent portfolio building service. They are very approachable yet professional and trustworthy. I am very happy to recommend Kam and his team at Premier Portfolio Builder."

ABOUT THE AUTHOR

Kam Dovedi

Kam Dovedi is a highly respected UK leading property expert. Kam has been investing for over 25 years and has built up a significant multi-million pound property portfolio resulting in financial freedom. Kam is an extremely dedicated, knowledgeable and experienced property specialist primarily focusing on the buy to let sector.

His passion for property is infectious and has allowed him to give back. Kam has been invited to speak on many stages nationally, has mentored over 100 successful property investors and is also the founder of Premier Portfolio Builder, one of the fastest growing property portfolio building companies specifically in the south east of England.

Kam has implemented these techniques he mentions in his book to maximise cash flow from single let properties – property let as a single unit – and achieved fantastic results.

Kam is an extremely dedicated, knowledgeable and experienced property specialist. He also has over two decades of experience in business organisation and development, and is the managing director of an import, export and distribution business with excellent processes and systems in place which he implements in his property business.

Due to this, Kam is able to help people at all levels to create wealth through property as an investment vehicle.

A PERSONAL STATEMENT BY THE AUTHOR

I believe that in our lifetimes, there is one moment which changes the pathway on which our futures are heading. That moment shapes our lives, and what actions we take from there are a cause of that moment. That moment came for me on 17th of February 2008, and on that day, my whole world changed. That moment was when my mother was diagnosed with that hated six-letter disease that many of our lives have been touched by.

In that moment of desperation, I made so many huge promises so that my mum could get better. I reached out to the universe and really asked for help. The amazing thing is when you really ask with all your heart, mind and soul, the 'universe' provides.

On February 17th 2008, I discovered my purpose.

I believe my purpose in life is to help people and give them hope, to serve people and add value to their lives, and that's what I promised that day.

I believe in a life of freedom, a life of choice, a life where we do not have to neglect our friends, families or desires because we are trading our time for money.

I believe in a life where we are the masters of our own lives.

Property is simply a vehicle that is allowing me to fulfil my purpose and mission. I love property, and it's something that I can do very well.

I am not in the property business just to make more money – I am grateful that I have more than enough, truly an abundance of what I need.

I am in this business to fulfil my purpose, and the more people I help, the larger my property business grows as a result, and the larger the financial gains are too. It is simply self-perpetuating.

If you have a skill, or gift in a certain craft, use it to the best of your ability. Property allows me to help everybody who comes into contact with me.

In that moment in 2008, my life changed. Today, my mum now lives in one of my half a million pound properties rent free and has no financial worries because my property portfolio takes care of that for her.

Today, I have a built a team, who share the same mission, vision and values as I do. This is the reason why we are the fastest-growing portfolio building company in the south east. It is because of the beliefs we share.

Today we have helped many people truly fulfil their lives through helping them to boost their pension and income, helping them create time so that they can live the life of their dreams.

The question that then remains is, how can my team and I serve you?

Kam Dovedi

34090627R00114

Made in the USA
Charleston, SC
30 September 2014